Strategic Insights

· ·

**DECISION-MAKING TOOLS
FOR BUSINESS LEADERS**

**Caryn Spain
and
Ron Wishnoff**

The Oasis Press®/PSI Research, Inc.
Central Point, Oregon

This publication is designed to provide accurate and authoritative information in regard to the subject matter covered. It is sold with the understanding that the author and publisher are not engaged in rendering legal, accounting, or other professional service. If legal advice or other expert assistance is required, the services of a competent professional person should be sought.
— *from a declaration of principles jointly adopted by a committee of the American Bar Association and a committee of publishers.*

Interior design by Eliot House Productions
Cover illustration and design by Steven Burns

Please direct any comments, questions, or suggestions regarding this book to The Oasis Press®/PSI Research:
Editorial Department
P.O. Box 3727
Central Point, OR 97502
(541) 245-6502
info@psi-research.com *e-mail*

The Oasis Press® is a Registered Trademark of Publishing Services, Inc., an Oregon corporation doing business as PSI Research.

Library of Congress Cataloging-in-Publication Data
Spain, Caryn, 1957-
    Strategic insights : decision-making tools for business leaders / Caryn Spain and Ron Wishnoff.-- 1st ed.
    p. cm.
    Includes index.
    ISBN 1-55571-505-2 (pbk.)
    1. Decision making. 2. Strategic plannig. I. Wishnoff, Ron. II. Title.

HD30.23 .S686 2000
658.4'012--dc21   00-029795

Printed in the United States of America
First Edition 10 9 8 7 6 5 4 3

 Printed on recycled paper when available

Contents

••

Contents

Introduction

∙∙

Our purpose in writing this book is to demonstrate and make more accessible our proven and easy-to-follow method for developing a viable and compelling business strategy and its related strategic plan. *Strategic Insights* provides the reader with decision-making tools for creating, strengthening, and maintaining a competitive advantage. Utilizing these tools results in valuable strategic insights and the formation of a unique business strategy.

This book reveals how to identify the basic elements of business strategy, apply those elements to your industry and business, and then combine them in new ways to see and actualize previously unknown strategies. An effective business strategy is the result of a comprehensive strategic decision-making process. We use the term strategic *decision-making* in place of strategic *planning* (as it is generally referred to) because good, solid *decision-making* powers your business forward and provides the momentum to achieve your Vision.

We have taken what once was a complex technique, simplified the terminology, and refined the procedures so they are easy to follow. By demystifying this highly effective boardroom practice and tailoring it to the realities of small and mid-size business, we give you a powerful tool for leading and developing your company.

Business strategy is the development and utilization of specific characteristics that set your business apart and provide you with an advantage over the competition. This book engages the reader in a dialogue about the different ways your business can differentiate itself from the competition. It gives you tools to answer one of the toughest business questions you will ever be asked: *Why would someone choose to buy products or services from your company versus the competition?*

We are small business owners ourselves. We have experienced the exhilaration and success that follows the implementation of a comprehensive and compelling business strategy. Through our personal and professional experiences, we understand how frustrating and unproductive it is to direct a business with no clear strategy or Vision in mind. In this book we show you how to answer the strategic questions that focus your operational initiatives, prioritize resource allocation, and position your business as unique in its industry. Our aim is to :

- ◈ Present business leaders with tools for developing a viable and compelling business Vision.

- ◈ Empower business leaders to see, understand, and evaluate their Strategic Choices.

- ◈ Clarify the role of strategic decision-making in transforming your business into a vessel for achieving your dreams.

- ◈ Demonstrate how to maximize your resources by making day-to-day decisions consistent with a single overriding principle, your Vision.

- ◈ Exemplify the insight other business leaders have received through the strategic decision-making process.

Many of our clients have successfully changed the direction of their businesses through strategic decision-making.

Instead of selling services by the hour, a mid-size engineering firm created a competitive advantage by linking their fees to their performance. They are now paid for their services based on their clients' direct return on investment (ROI) over the next ten years. They have clearly distinguished themselves from the competition and are now in the annuities business.

A small landscape contractor was struggling to break out of smaller, less profitable jobs to larger, high-end projects. They repositioned the company as the premier firm to manage the installation of exquisite, high-end landscapes. The new focus on design and contract management freed up their resources and staff so they could pursue more of the projects that match their Vision.

A regional brass foundry was faced with the consolidation of their distributors. They chose to remain independent, increase their foundry capacity, modernize their manufacturing processes, and become a major international distributor of a full line of products.

A full service estimating and construction management firm realized that our prosperous economy was forcing them to grow in ways that were neither desirable nor sustainable in the long-term. The owners wanted to take back control and keep the company small, focused, and profitable. They used strategic decision-making to identify the parts of their work they preferred and which were more profitable and less risky. The result was the development of a new specialty niche and increased owner satisfaction.

There are many experts, consultants, and books available to give you advice on what you should do next with your business. We do not presume to know what is best for *your* business. Strategic decision-making provides you with a systematic method for making your own decisions. You, the business leader, are the only one who can envision your Strategic Choices and choose the right course for your business.

Much of the advice available in the marketplace offers recommendations on *how* to move more efficiently toward your goals. Whether it is quality management, re-engineering, just-in-time inventory practices, management skills, open-book accounting, employee involvement, or any of the thousands of other tools available. This operational advice is only helpful *after* you have already defined where your business is going. Operational advice can take you off course if you have not first clearly defined your Vision and your purposes for being in business.

You may also be interested in *Chart Your Own Course®*, the companion volume to this book. It is written in a workbook format to facilitate the development and implementation of your strategic plan. It is also the seminar guide for our *Chart Your Own Course®* Executive Seminars and Retreats.

Getting Started

The first three chapters discuss the definitions of, relationships between, and benefits to be gained by understanding business strategy, participating in strategic decision-making, and utilizing a strategic plan. The remaining chapters detail the steps required to make strategic decision-making work for you, and how you can apply it to your business.

Strategic decision-making is a comprehensive process for choosing the best course for you *and* your business. It is a method for generating a variety of viable strategic choices and applying the appropriate criteria for selecting an effective strategy. Ultimately, the purpose of strategic decision-making is to position your business as unique in its industry, clarify your core purpose as a business, and define what actions you must take to develop and maintain your competitive advantage. The decisions you make, and the logic and assumptions that led up to them, are recorded in an easily referenced, living document called a strategic plan. Ideally your strategic plan is revisited quarterly and revised annually.

Throughout this book we use sailing and navigational metaphors to help the business leader appreciate that running a business is very much like undertaking a voyage. Like a boat, your business operates in a constantly changing environment. There are predictable currents and, even more importantly, there are very unpredictable situations that your vessel may be forced to deal with. The strategic decision-making process is designed to engage the business leader and his or her crew in deciding on the destination (before you leave the dock), charting the best course, and keeping a vigilant watch. Your strategic plan helps you anticipate and respond to the ever-changing business environment and serves as a guide to all subsequent day-to-day (operational) decision-making.

Our (Not Too) Hidden Agenda

Our not too hidden agenda for writing this book is to help you the reader become a visionary business leader. Our objective is for you to be able to see a unique business strategy — a Vision, a previously unknown, yet compelling, picture of what is possible in your industry. As much as anything else this book is a step-by-step demonstration of the art of visioning.

When you use this book to adjust your business' course so that it fulfills your Personal Definition of Success, builds on your Core Capabilities, limits the competition, and meets forecasted market needs we will have achieved a great accomplishment. If, in addition, you maximize these tools to their fullest potential, if you truly "look outside the boxes," if you keep exploring until you see a strategy that no one has ever seen before, then we will have succeeded in a way that few before us ever have.

The easiest way to choose a strategy is to copy an already existing one. For example, once McDonalds demonstrated that a restaurant could be successful by mass-producing hamburgers, then others copied that strategy. Once AmWay demonstrated that a company could be successful utilizing multi-level marketing, then they too were copied. Once Amazon.com demonstrated the power of e-commerce, others in their industry were quick to copy. However, copying is one of the more difficult strategies to be successful with for the simple reason that you are always following, and from that position it is both difficult to see and difficult to win. The tools we lay out for you reveal how great insight can be gained by going beyond known and familiar territories.

As the leader of your business, your primary responsibility is to take the helm and chart a course to success. Strategic decision-making tools reveal the right course for you *and* your business. Our mission is to enhance your business' success. Our straight-forward approach has proven highly beneficial for people like you and us — business leaders who are committed to realizing our personal and professional dreams. We challenge you to take the helm.

Bon Voyage!

— Caryn A. Spain C.M.C. and Captain Ron Wishnoff

Issues, Challenges, and Opportunities

Choosing where to lead your business is one of the toughest and most important decisions a business leader is responsible for making. As business leaders, everyday we are faced with issues, challenges, and opportunities. Pro-actively addressing those challenges and choosing the right opportunities to pursue, in a manner consistent with a single over-riding principle, is the purpose of strategic decision-making.

Bob Inkman, like you, is a successful entrepreneur. He works hard, makes a good living, and is looking for a way to transition out of his business someday and receive a good return on the investment he has made during his career with his company.

Bob owns a small print shop and has been in business for 15 years. He is standing at what feels like a crossroads. He is tired of working so hard and sees dramatic changes in his industry, as well as lots of opportunities for a business leader who is willing to invest. Bob is not sure what to do next. The major challenges and opportunities that Bob sees today include:

◆ *Investing in technology and keeping up with the industry.* An investment in technology would require he find financing and grow the business significantly to justify and pay off the increased investment. Bob is not sure if he has the energy to grow his business or if he is positioned correctly to compete for the increased market share he would need to pay off the investment.

◆ *Forming a partnership or strategic alliance with some smaller competitors.* This could be a way to better position the company in order to compete with the national franchises. Together, they reason, they could pool their resources, increase everyone's market exposure, and maximize their combined equipment and production capability by creating shared resources. In addition, this could help pool the capital needed to buy the newer equipment required to compete.

◆ *Diversifying the business and moving towards a more full-service printing business.* Mel, one of Bob's newest staff members, brought significant experience in desktop publishing with him when he joined the firm. Now the old print clients are using Mel to provide their prepress services, and the desktop publishing department is starting to show significant promise as a new profit center for the company. Bob wonders if he should invest in more design and layout people, to become a more full-service printing business.

◆ *Changing his company's market niche.* Bob's current equipment is no longer big enough or fast enough to compete on many of the private sector jobs he used to consider his bread and butter. As a result, he has noticed that his clients are changing in composition and demographics. He now provides services to a lot of small nonprofits and social organizations, as well as the community colleges in his area. He wonders if he should beef up his marketing dollars for more private sector jobs or focus his commitment and his marketing efforts in the area of nonprofits.

◆ *Becoming a subcontractor for larger companies.* An alternative strategy his peers have suggested is to position his business to be a subcontractor to other printing companies who are looking to farm out their long run, lower quality, two-color production projects.

◆ *Growing the business management end of the business.* Bob's son just completed his MBA and is interested in the business end of the business, but not the printing. In order for the business to be big enough to support both the father and son as business managers they would need to grow the business significantly. Bob's son has developed a plan to create a franchise and market it nationally to other small print shops that are in a similar position to them.

Aren't you glad you're not in the same position as Bob? Or are you? Many companies are faced with these kinds of challenges and opportunities due to changes in the marketplace, internal company issues, new competition, technological advances, and ever-evolving personal goals. A snapshot of any business leader's life often finds him or her at a crossroads. Navigating a successful business requires consistent decision-making. Take a few minutes to identify the opportunities and challenges you are exploring. Worksheet 1 helps you clarify and organize your thoughts about the issues, challenges, and opportunities your business is presently faced with.

Business leaders need tools to quickly grasp the potential impact of opportunities such as:

◆ Selling the business.

◆ Merging with partners from another industry.

◆ Developing new products.

◆ Investing in equipment, technology, or human resources.

◆ Powering your way to capture more market share.

Strategic decision-making is a way of considering multiple factors and opportunities while appreciating the potential future impact of each set of choices. Because the factors you need to take into consideration are often large in number and varied in

Navigating a successful business requires consistent decision-making.

WORKSHEET 1: Issues, Challenges, and Opportunities

What are the challenges you face that require you to consider a new course for your business?

_____

_____

What differentiates you today from your competition?

_____

_____

What are the opportunities you are, or have been, considering investing in?

_____

_____

What are the opportunities others have suggested you consider investing in?

_____

_____

What are others in your industry investing in?

_____

_____

What have you recently invested in to better position your business for ongoing success?

_____

_____

What kind of exit strategy (from your business) have you envisioned for yourself?

_____

_____

importance we have developed this linear, logical, data-driven approach. Ultimately, the purpose of strategic decision-making is to differentiate your business and clarify your core purpose as a business, as well as define what actions you must take to develop and maintain your competitive advantage. The decisions you make, and the logic and assumptions that led up to them, are recorded in an easily referenced strategic plan that can be updated and used to guide all subsequent day-to-day (operational) decision-making.

Although strategic decision-making is primarily concerned with the strategic (big picture) issues facing your company, by addressing your strategic issues it creates a context for answering your important operational questions. Both strategic and operational issues are addressed in this comprehensive strategic decision-making process.

Are You a Business *Owner* or Business *Leader*

The responsibility for making strategic decisions is the sole province of the business owner and/or executive management team. You are the captain of your ship. Must you shoulder this responsibility alone? No. Strategic decision-making is a four-stage process. Stages One and Two are ideal opportunities to include your management team and partner(s), and to elicit advice from your spouse or other trusted advisers. Stages Three and Four are the ideal place to include feedback from a broader spectrum of employees and customers/prospects.

It is often more comfortable for business owners to put out fires on a daily basis than to design their businesses to be less flammable.

These are important decisions and as a result are sometimes difficult to make. It is often more comfortable for business owners to put out fires on a daily basis than to design their businesses to be less flammable. The difference between a business *owner* and a business *leader* is that the business *leader* looks forward and proactively charts the best course available to his or her business. Does this guarantee success? Of course not, but it significantly increases your chances of arriving at your destination if you know what you're looking for!

We agree wholeheartedly with Michael Gerber who, in his book *The E-Myth*, speaks about how business leaders need to stop working *in* their businesses long enough to start working *on* their businesses. Working *on* your business is the focus of strategic decision-making. Taking the step from business *owner* to *leader* requires looking up from your desk and proactively addressing the challenges and opportunities that directly impact your business.

Benefits of Strategic Decision-Making

The benefits of taking the time to define your business strategy are:

- Find innovative ways to provide an established product or service.
- Clarify conflicting priorities and evaluate new opportunities.
- Streamline and focus your marketing efforts.
- Transform your business into a vessel for achieving your dreams.

Find Innovative Ways to Provide an Established Product or Service

Strategic decision-making helps you expand your thinking about what is possible for your business.

Back in 1899, a common saying was, "Everything that can be invented has already been invented." Whomever said it couldn't have been more wrong. Even though not everyone can invent a brand-new product or service, each of us has the opportunity to:

- Reinvent an old product or service in a new way.
- Find a new market niche or application for a current product.
- Find a new way to sell or deliver a product or service.

Strategic decision-making helps you expand your thinking about what is possible for your business. For example, what set

SeaLand apart from their competitors was not that they were in the transportation business, but that they found "a new way" to be in the transportation business. They led the industry by providing standardized containers that did not need to be unpacked and repacked when they were transferred from sea to land.

Each of us can discover a unique way to provide our products or services by exploring both charted and uncharted options during our strategic explorations. You need to consider at least ten new ways to be in business before you will have the confidence to say that you really looked strategically at your business opportunities. In today's business environment, most of us do not have totally unique products or services. One way to carve out a market niche then is to find a new way to offer already established products or services. Some examples are:

> You need to consider at least ten new ways to be in business, before you will have the confidence to say that you really looked strategically at your business opportunities.

- ◆ Amway took household supplies to a new level by establishing a multi-level marketing network.

- ◆ Disney took entertainment to a multi-dimensional level by offering huge entertainment parks.

- ◆ Evian opened a whole new beverage market by offering consumers personal sized bottled water in convenience stores.

- ◆ Worksite Massage reinvigorated the massage industry. They offer massage bars at airports and office buildings around the country.

- ◆ Homegrocer.com is a new way of provisioning your kitchen. You choose your groceries online and they deliver them for free.

- ◆ FedEx just joined the Postal Service in a public/private partnership to deliver products purchased through e-commerce.

Use the strategic decision-making process to explore uncharted territories and reveal previously unknown ways of providing your products and services.

Clarify Conflicting Priorities
and Evaluate New Opportunities

Strategic decision-making is a tool to evaluate and select opportunities, clarify existing priorities, and learn to say no to the distractions that can blow you off course. The more successful you are, the more opportunities will present themselves. This can be very exciting. Unfortunately trying to take advantage of too many or the wrong opportunities can be a business' undoing. Once you appreciate that you cannot be all things to all people you start recognizing the importance of prioritizing.

We were working with a world class architectural firm which reported that 40 percent of their work was the projects they had specifically targeted, projects they had expertise in and had built their reputation on. The remaining 60 percent of their work is "opportunity work" — people coming to them with projects that they agreed to design.

When asked why they didn't have more of their target projects, they reported they didn't have enough human resources to look for the right projects, develop relationships with prospects, or write proposals. Why didn't they have the resources? Because those resources were too busy doing the "opportunity work." A clear strategy in hand gives you the confidence to say no to the demands and distractions that try to blow you off course.

> A clear strategy in hand gives you the confidence to say no to the demands and distractions that try to blow you off course.

Many of us are operating our businesses at least half on "opportunity projects." We continue to sell products that provide us with cash flow but don't add momentum to achieving a long-term Vision. We try to maneuver our business but are slowed down by dead weight we are unwilling to unload. To make room for the work that this architectural firm really wants to do they will have to start saying no to the work they do not want, thus freeing up the needed resources. It's about as easy for small business owners to say *no* to work as it is to write tax checks with a smile. The confidence, the power to say *no* results from completing a comprehensive strategic decision-making process and having a plan in place to get more of the right work.

A small convenience store continues to offer everything from espresso, curios, and snack foods to fishing gear, while they do not have the capital to purchase more of the inventory that really makes them money. An engineering firm continues to take restoration projects because they have a past relationship with the building owners, even though they know they do not have the staff expertise or the time to address the needs of these specialized projects in a profitable manner. A small insurance company offers every kind of insurance and feels secure because they are completely diversified; however, they do not have the market share today to justify developing the systems required to effectively service each type of account.

Many businesses are squandering their resources by servicing the wrong projects while at the same time screaming for additional room, staff, and resources. It is important to get your vessel completely above water before undertaking an aggressive new journey. This may entail saying "no" to some of your current work, work that is not providing you with the momentum you need to achieve your Vision.

Streamline and Focus Your Marketing Initiatives

When asked who their target markets are business owners often respond by saying "everyone." Focusing in on your ideal target market and your highest priority products or services will maximize your marketing dollars, and increase the effectiveness of all your marketing efforts.

Different customers are attracted to different business strategies. Your strategy determines in general who will be attracted to your services or products. Knowing whom you are attracting to your business strategy, and investing your marketing energy and dollars to gain exposure with that market, increases your return on investment and streamlines your marketing efforts.

A small payroll and human resource administration company identified the following characteristics, which formed the foundation of a powerful business strategy.

> Many businesses are squandering their resources by servicing the wrong projects while at the same time screaming for additional room, staff, and resources.

- Provide a full range of human resource administration functions, including payroll, performance management, compensation, and benefits analysis.

- Apply leading-edge technology to increase operational efficiency.

- Develop strategic alliances with other firms offering out-sourced human resource services, including temporary and placement agencies.

- Retain customer accounts by building a reliance on their human resources administration.

They selected these characteristics because together they form a solid Vision and create a competitive advantage. The business described by this strategy offers appealing payroll/human resource solutions to many prospects and customers, but of course, not to all. The next step in their process is to use this Vision to identify the clients most likely to be attracted to this unique combination of characteristics.

The company used their current client list to identify which of their customers were most attracted to their new strategy, and who relied on them for ongoing human resource administration functions. With this short list of "ideal clients" in hand, they were able to do another level of analysis. They analyzed the list to discover the qualities and profiles that all (or most) these "ideal clients" share. They discovered that the companies most attracted to their strategy were in traditional industries, with conservative growth, and privately owned. Appreciating the profile of their target market, from the perspective of their selected business strategy, enabled them to better focus their marketing efforts as well as their marketing message.

When they began to operationalize their strategy they discovered that their sales representatives invested a lot of time talking with the more glamorous high-tech firms, and were predisposed to joining local high-tech professional associations. Even though high-tech is one of the fastest growing and sexiest sectors in their community, they had learned that high-tech companies were not particularly attracted to the strategy they had chosen. They refocused their marketing efforts to better reach their true target market.

After a little research they learned that their target market was actively involved in community civic organizations like Rotary and Kiwanis, as well as nonprofit boards. Armed with this insight they developed new performance standards for their sales force, which included getting actively involved in these organizations where they gained visibility and were able to develop relationships with their true target market. They were then able to focus and streamline their marketing initiatives to spend the majority of their dollars and energy contacting prospects that best match their target market customers who are drawn to their business strategy.

Without a clear business strategy your marketing efforts will be scattered or focused on the wrong target. Having a comprehensive business strategy and following it through to focus on an "ideal customer profile" or target market will quickly strengthen and streamline your marketing efforts.

Transforming Your Business into a Vessel for Achieving Your Dreams

When you first started your business, simply being in business for yourself may have been the goal. You were working for someone else and wanted more freedom or felt you could "do it better" on your own, or an irresistible opportunity to get in business for yourself came along. However, once you achieve some financial stability, it is again time to look at your purpose for *being* in business. Many successful business owners have reached a plateau and are looking for ways to take their businesses to the next level.

It is Saturday, and the rest of the world is taking the weekend off. But for you it seems there is always something more to do, another marketing or public relations idea to pursue, a customer demand that couldn't be met during the week, or a proposal to write. We all know running any business requires work, discipline, and doing things you may not want to do. It doesn't matter

> Without a clear business strategy your marketing efforts will be scattered or focused on the wrong target.

if you own a tortilla distributorship, a Subway franchise, or a law firm. Business ownership and management require a lot of work, long hours, and discipline. Hard work is the nature of business leadership. So why sail in circles when you can use that hard work to propel you towards your preferred future?

....

Business ownership and management require a lot of work, long hours, and discipline.

You invest a significant amount of time, energy, and money in your business. Too much time, energy, and money to squander going in circles. Design your business to be a vessel, or vehicle, for achieving your personal goals and dreams. The first step is to explore the question: where do you want this vessel to take you?

Some business leaders find themselves in business simply to make a living and have identified their business and industry as a viable way of doing so. These business owners may be looking for strategies that help reduce their work, time commitment, and the resources required to maintain their business, while still ensuring it is generating an income.

Other business leaders are driven by their businesses. Their personal identities, and much of their satisfaction in life, are tied to the visible success of their businesses. This type of business leader is often driven to make the business bigger, better, more visible. These business owners require a different strategy.

Exit strategies, and succession plans have become hot topics over the past few years as many baby boomer entrepreneurs are preparing to retire. These businesses also require a different strategy. To be successful, exit strategies should be set in place at least five years in advance.

Does your picture of success include selling the business, creating a part time job for yourself, generating residual or passive income, or passing the business on to your children or employees? Each of these goals requires setting a slightly different course for your business today. The sooner you set the right course, the sooner you will get there.

Some business leaders have created a business that is fulfilling. Doing the work itself provides the individual with a sense of personal satisfaction. These business leaders are often interested in strategies to maintain current levels of success without adding additional pressures or outside influences.

Of course, there is often a little of these types of business owners in most of us. One day we want to grow our business, go national, and see ourselves as prominent business leaders. The next day you envy the business owner who goes on extended vacations, and her business, while not growing or highly visible, is easily maintained through good systems and strong people. The next day you think about growing the business so it will pay high dividends when you are ready to retire. Integrating your personal requirements and goals into your business decision-making process can lead to a unique business strategy, personal satisfaction, and the realization of your financial goals.

The managing partner of a regional accounting firm complains about the responsibility of managing a CPA firm in such a turbulent environment. The whole CPA industry is re-engineering itself in response to aggressive mergers and acquisitions. Traditional compliance-based tax services are becoming obsolete as many CPA roles are being replaced by software solutions. The managing partner, when asked about his personal goals, indicates he would prefer to have a self-managing business that is able to maintain itself with minimal leadership six months of the year — the six months when the owner would prefer to be at his beach cottage with his family. However, when asked about his business Vision, he immediately starts talking about growing the number and complexity of services they offer. He plans to expand his full-time staff, hire more consultants, and move into a larger, high visibility office building. What is wrong with this picture? He is building a business that will take him in the exact opposite direction from his personal definition of success.

A business can be a vehicle for achieving any number of personal goals, including increasing your personal reputation and name recognition, creating a job you love, and increasing the equity in your business for a future sale, franchise or license.

Unfortunately, some people do not believe their profession can be enjoyable or meaningful. They have not experienced the

> Integrating your personal requirements and goals into your business decision-making process can lead to a unique business strategy, personal satisfaction, and the realization of your financial goals.

boost in motivation and energy associated with transforming your business into a vessel for achieving your dreams. Your dreams and Vision are what give you the energy and stamina you need to go the extra mile, to continue when everyone else has quit, and to hold on through the difficult times. You can invest your time, energy, and money without clear direction, or you can focus your efforts to achieve your dreams. Strategic decision-making clarifies exactly what it is you want to achieve.

Strategy Versus Operations

It is important to appreciate the relationship and distinctions between strategy and operations. *Strategy* focuses your attention on where you want your business to be five to ten years from now. *Operations* are the specific steps required to get your business there. To paraphrase Peter Drucker, effectiveness is about doing the *right work*, efficiency is about doing the *work right*. When you are thinking strategically, you are answering questions associated with your company's effectiveness — thereby clarifying which is the *right work* for your company. Operational planning answers questions associated with your company's efficiency.

When business leaders look only for opportunities to increase efficiency, without a clear direction of where they are headed, they often miss the most effective way to position the business. In his book *On Competition*, Michael Porter speaks eloquently and at length on how the pursuit of operational efficiencies, no matter how successful, cannot, by themselves, provide a sustainable competitive advantage. Remember to always answer the strategic questions before the operational questions.

Your business is a vehicle, a vessel for getting somewhere. And like a vessel on the ocean, your business moves through an environment that constantly changes. However, most business owners don't realize they are already underway without a clear destination in mind. Strategic decision-making is concerned with defining your destination. Operational decision-making focuses you on the mechanics of getting there. Addressing the

When business leaders look only for opportunities to increase efficiency, without a clear direction of where they are headed, they often miss the most effective way to position the business.

WORKSHEET 2: Assess Your Preference: Strategy or Operations

Try the following, fun exercise; assess your preference as a business leader for addressing operations versus strategy.

Starting with the letter W or an H (such as why or how), write down seven words that begin questions.

	Strategic Questions	Operational Questions
1. _____	_____	_____
2. _____	_____	_____
3. _____	_____	_____
4. _____	_____	_____
5. _____	_____	_____
6. _____	_____	_____
7. _____	_____	_____

strategic questions first is as important as agreeing on your ship's course *before* you leave the dock. Try Worksheet 2 to see whether you prefer strategy or operations.

Did you get all seven? If you did not, it is likely a strategic question that you have overlooked. It is often easier to remember the operational question words — the questions that help determine *who* will do *what* by *when*. Some of the words that start questions point your thoughts toward strategic issues, while others point you toward operational issues. Take a moment to consider and mark which question words focus your mind on strategic versus operational issues.

....

A challenging
component for success
in the strategic decision-
making process
therefore lies in
reorienting business
leaders to focus on
answering the strategic
questions first.

Most people come up with the first six words when completing Worksheet 2. The *which* question is the one most often forgotten, or written down last. Though often overlooked, the *which* question is the most strategic question of all. The majority of business leaders are more comfortable with operations than they are with strategy. This makes sense. Most likely you got to where you are today through your technical expertise, i.e., you were (and are) a star performer in your industry or field. But the skills of a star performer are not necessarily the same skills needed by a business leader. A missing *which* question on your list is indicative of your emphasis on operations versus strategy.

A challenging component for success in the strategic decision-making process therefore lies in reorienting business leaders to focus on answering the strategic questions first.

The reason the *which* questions are often missed is the preference for operations. This is also evident in the desire to make quick decisions that will have an immediate effect. This preference for operations can cause executives to act like managers, and managers to micro-manage. The two question words that focus on strategic decisions are *which* and *why*. The process of strategic decision-making begins with analyzing and prioritizing your choices (which), then justifying (why) you made those choices.

	Strategic Questions	Operational Questions
1. Who		X
2. What		X
3. Where		X
4. When		X
5. Why	X	
6. How		X
7. Which	X	

The five strategic decisions all businesses face are:

1. Why are we in business?
2. Which business should we be in?
3. Which customers should we serve?
4. Which products or services should we offer?
5. Why have we decided on this focus?

The five operational decisions all businesses face are:

1. What areas require that we set goals?
2. How should we achieve our goals?
3. When should we achieve our goals?
4. Where should we focus our resources?
5. Who should be responsible to achieve our goals?

Is it possible to simultaneously implement all the opportunities you identified in the Worksheet 1? No. This is where the *which* question comes into play. Strategic decision-making is a tool for prioritizing and integrating business opportunities into a comprehensive strategy that makes good business sense.

Think about the *which* questions you are presently faced with. For most business leaders there are many *which* questions. Any question that requires choosing between two or more competing demands or opportunities is inherently a *which* question. The following are some examples of company-specific strategic (*which*) business questions.

- Resources are limited. Should we invest in technology or hire additional people?
- We are in the start-up mode. Should we try to sell our services for less to generate business or go after a higher-price market position?
- Will it be better to form a strategic alliance or remain independent?
- Should we add new product lines or remain specialized?

Any question that requires choosing between two or more competing demands or opportunities is inherently a which question.

Navigate Using Four Key Perspectives

....

You want to be confident that the direction you choose is the right one.

Choosing the right direction and defining your company's ultimate destination can feel like an overwhelming task. You want to be confident that the direction you choose is the right one. This is especially true once you appreciate that your business strategy forms the foundation for much of your day-to-day decision-making. The most important characteristics of any foundation are strength and stability.

To be strong and stable your strategy should take into account several perspectives. Developing an effective business strategy is best accomplished by considering your business, and the choices available to you, from four key perspectives. Those four key perspectives are:

- *The business owner's Personal Definition of Success.* Don't assume that your Personal Definition of Success (PDS) is the same as the guy's next door. Inspire, energize, and motivate yourself by aligning your business strategy with your personal values and goals. As an added bonus, many business leaders have found a way to use their PDS to further differentiate the business from the competition.

- *A data-driven Market Forecast.* No financial enterprise can move forward with confidence without having some idea of what to expect in terms of changing market needs and other important factors that impact the way you do business. The Market Forecast makes, and keeps you aware of, the direction your industry is headed in and what changes you will need to anticipate in the market at large.

- *A Competitive Analysis.* Not all businesses within the same industry compete directly with each other. The Competitive Analysis enlightens you to the strategies that your competition is using, and *not* using. Selecting a strategy that your competition is not using, or using well, can provide you with a distinct competitive advantage.

- *Core Capabilities.* Take advantage, and make the most, of the hard work you have put in to bring your business to where it is today. It is essential, and simple common sense, to build your business strategy on the Core Capabilities, qualities, and characteristics that are the source of your business' current success.

A good strategy is constructed like a pyramid. The pyramid is the most stable structure ever engineered by man. The strategy pyramid in Figure 1.1 shows how the four key perspectives form the foundation of business strategy and acts like an arrow pointing towards a viable and compelling business Vision.

FIGURE 1.1: Use Four Perspectives to Define Your Business Strategy

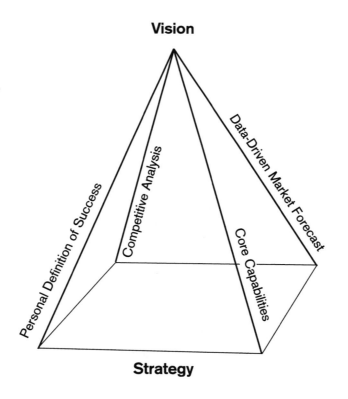

Strategic Decision-Making Requires Time and Perspective

....

Looking at the big picture is not effectively sandwiched between day-to-day operations, addressed late on Friday afternoons, or contemplated in short sound bites.

Strategic navigation requires looking at the big picture from several perspectives. It is helpful to find some longer periods of uninterrupted time to consider your choices and think about the future. Looking at the big picture is not effectively sandwiched between day-to-day operations, addressed late on Friday afternoons, or contemplated in short sound bites. It is a good idea to set some time apart to gain perspective.

Perspective is gained by removing yourself from the demands of your daily workload to survey the marketplace, assess your competition, consider your capabilities, and clarify your personal objectives for being in business. You will find that strategic planning and decision-making will be more productive when you provide yourself with longer blocks of time, use a disciplined and orderly approach, and anticipate the steps required to turn your Vision into Action. You may also find it valuable to attend a strategic decision-making retreat.

Strategic Decision-Making requires:

- The time and distance to gain perspective from day-to-day operations.
- A commitment to telling the truth about your personal needs and expectations.
- The discipline to follow a simple, yet structured, thought process and the patience to look at the future from multiple perspectives before making your final decision.
- An open and creative mind that is willing to see opportunities not already discovered or demonstrated in your industry.
- Gathering data to test or confirm your knowledge and intuitive guesses about the future business environment.
- Honest evaluation of your company's current position, strengths, and weaknesses.

Strategic Decision-Making is a four-stage process. Chapter 2 lays out in detail the four stages.

Four Stages to Turn Your Vision Into Action

Vision without Action is merely a dream. Action without Vision simply passes the time. Vision with Action can change the world.

Strategic decision-making is a four-stage process that guides you from creating the big-picture Vision of where you are headed all the way through to the specific operational decisions and account-abilities needed to turn your Vision into Action. Each stage requires a decision, which then results in a step towards comple-tion of your strategic plan. The first two stages focus on the strate-gic decisions and the second two stages focus on the operational decisions. This method, in its simplest terms, has the reader define point "B" (where you want your business to be five to ten years from now) before returning to point "A" (where it is today), and then chart a course to get from Point "A" to point "B."

A • Stages Three and Four define Point A — where your business is today.

Stages One and Two define Point B — where you B want your business to be five years from now.

....

A visionary thinker is an individual who has developed the cognitive capability to see how multiple factors interact, based on different variables, over a longer time horizon.

The process outlined in this book is similar to the way a strategic or visionary thinker would naturally envision the future. A visionary thinker is an individual who has developed the cognitive capability to see how multiple factors interact, based on different variables, over a longer time horizon. Not everyone is a visionary thinker. However, we have mapped out the steps in the visionary thinking process and present them in a straightforward process that the reader can use to enhance their ability to visualize their preferred future.

Complete each stage before progressing to the next. The logic builds upon itself and is applied to the following stage to provide continuity, confidence, and clarity in the whole plan. If you are ever unsure as to where you stand in the process, refer to the four-stage strategic decision-making flowchart. The flowchart (Figure 2.1) is an excellent guide and will help you stay on course throughout this book.

The Four Stages for Turning Your Vision Into Action

- Stage One: Strategy. The result from working through this stage is a business strategy and Vision for your company.

- Stage Two: Focus. In light of your Vision, what are your top priority products/services and who precisely is your target market? The results of Stage Two decisions are summarized in your company's Mission.

- Stage Three: Assess Current Position. This stage begins the operationalization of your business strategy. The result is a survey of your current position and setting of goals.

- Stage Four: Operationalize. This stage defines the accountabilities in the form of Specific, Measurable, Agreed-upon, Realistic, with a Tracking system (SMART), result-oriented, objectives. The result is an agreement on who will do what by when, and the integration of your strategic plan with your company's budget.

By working through each stage, you will build the confidence and clarity you need to invest your company's resources on the achievement of your business Vision and define the best course

FIGURE 2.1: Strategic Decision-Making Flowchart

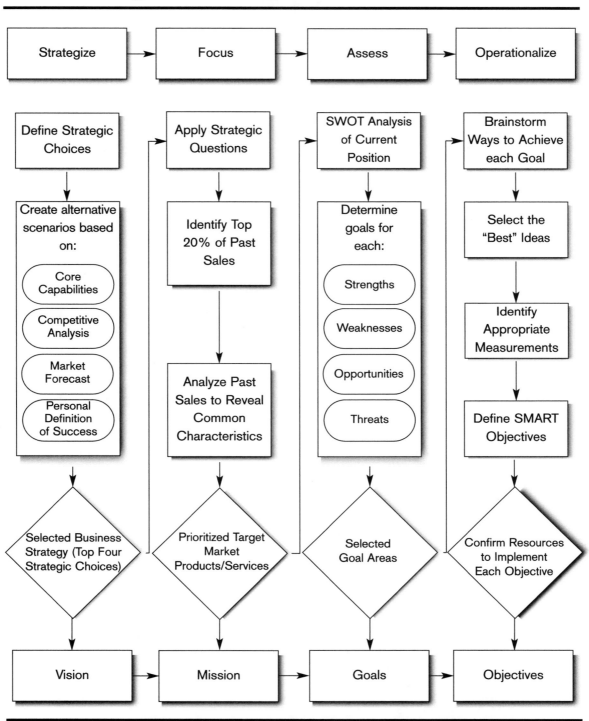

for your company. Each stage should be explored fully in order to arrive at the best plan of action for your company.

Stage One: Strategy

In Stage One it is important to appreciate and generate Strategic Choices for your company. These choices are the result of seeing how specific characteristics can be turned into a competitive advantage for your business. Your Strategic Choices represent the elements of a business strategy that can be combined and recombined to help you see new strategies for your business. This process is akin to looking through a kaleidoscope. A kaleidoscope uses a consistent set of elements. Each time you turn the lens those elements are recombined and result in the creation of a uniquely different image. Once you have clarified your Strategic Choices, we suggest you start looking at them from different perspectives. This means looking at your business and the opportunities available to you from different angles. The Strategic Choices that make good business sense when seen from more than one perspective are combined to form your business strategy and the Vision that results from it.

A Vision is a visual picture of what your business will look like five to ten years from now if you consistently invest in your selected and prioritized Strategic Choices. Your Vision statement is a motivational, internal, document that summarizes your strategic decisions and core purpose for being in business, and helps everyone in the company stay focused on your priorities and where your business is headed.

Stage Two: Focus

In Stage Two we discuss how you can use your business strategy to bring your target market into focus. We suggest you review your historical sales data and product list and identify the top 20 percent of your current clients, products, and services that provide the most momentum in achieving your Vision. This process will give you insight into the characteristics of your "ideal" target market and which of your products/services are most important to offer them. The decisions required at the end of

> Your Strategic Choices represent the elements of a business strategy that can be combined and recombined to help you see new strategies for your business.

Stage Two are: which part of the market should we focus on and which services/products should we offer? The results are summarized in your Mission.

A Mission statement is a concise answer to the question, "What does your Company do?" It states who your target market is, what your priority services are, and how you provide those services that distinguish you from the competition. It is a public statement, which is designed to attract your target market by having them recognize themselves and their needs, as well as the benefits of using your company to address their needs. Since it is the best answer to the question: "What do you do?" all staff should consistently use the Mission statement when describing the company, and it should be used in all literature and correspondence regarding the company.

Stage Three: Assess Current Position

This is where the operational planning begins. We use a traditional Strengths, Weaknesses, Opportunities, and Threats or SWOT assessment to identify the strengths, weaknesses, opportunities, and threats that must be addressed for you to actualize your strategy, reach your target market, and achieve your Vision. The decision required at the end of Stage Three answers the question: Which areas do we need to focus our attention on in order to achieve our Vision? The results are summarized into five to seven goal areas. It is interesting to note that some so-called strategic planning models actually begin with the creation of goals. However, setting goals and objectives without first clearly defining your business strategy and Vision is often a waste of valuable resources.

Goals are areas requiring operational emphasis (time, energy, and resources) in order to achieve the Vision and Mission. Most businesses already have sales and profit goals. In addition, businesses should have five or six operational goals to ensure they are retaining their current strengths, and addressing any operational weaknesses that impact their ability to achieve their Vision and Mission. Goals are in place for a two to five year time period.

The decision required at the end of Stage Three answers the question: Which areas do we need to focus our attention on in order to achieve our Vision?

Stage Four: Operationalize

Stage Four details the specific actions and results you expect to achieve over the next budget cycle. It is the final "reality check" within the strategic decision-making process. In Stage Four we suggest you identify what you specifically intend to achieve over the next 12 months, estimate the cost of implementing each objective, clarify realistic timetables, and assign accountability for turning your Vision into Action. The amount of resources you choose to invest impacts how quickly you can turn your Vision into Action. The decision required at the end of Stage Four answers the question: Which results can we realistically achieve this financial year? These results are your business objectives for the next 12 months.

Objectives are the specific, measurable results you are committed to achieving in the next 12 months in order to achieve each goal. There are generally two to five objectives for each goal. Each objective has a point person who is accountable for facilitating its achievement, as well as coordinating the budget and the schedule required to achieve the objective. The achievement of each annual objective marks progress towards fulfillment of your business goals and ultimately your business Vision.

Strategic Decision-Making Terminology

. . . .

The four distinct deliverables that a business leader receives from working through a strategic decision-making process are: a vision, mission, goals, and objectives.

What is the difference between a strategy, a tactic, a vision, a goal, and an objective? Unfortunately in the management consulting industry the answer more often than not is: "the consultant you use." We have tried whenever possible to define, clarify, and use the most commonly applied strategic planning terminology. The four distinct deliverables that a business leader receives from working through a strategic decision-making process are: a Vision, Mission, goals, and objectives. Our four-stage process moves your thinking from a general picture of where your business is headed (the Vision) to a very specific statement of who you expect to do what by when — your business objectives.

The power of a well-defined Vision and Mission cannot be underestimated. The strategic decisions you make in Stages One and Two are summarized in your Vision and Mission. They describe your ultimate destination and guide your passage. Many businesses already have Vision and Mission statements, but what do those statements really reflect? A frank review of the development of those statements often reveals little substantive decision-making, but instead these statements simply reflect the results of a brainstorming or teambuilding exercise. A clear and effective Vision or Mission should be the result of a comprehensive strategic decision-making process.

An example of this is a second-generation business leader who knew when he took charge that his staff's first expectation was to know his business Vision. He didn't really have one so they worked together for a day to create a shared Vision. They tried to write a Vision that included everyone's motivations and expectations, but they were unable to include everything without causing others to feel offended or left out. They decided to *just write a Mission statement instead*. Again they had little luck finding the right words. Finally they chose to just use their long time marketing slogan, "Contributing to our customers' success." It worked perfectly because it really didn't say anything, so it could offend no one, and it didn't leave anyone out either. But what value does this exercise provide the company? Too many business consultants have done a disservice to their clients by building motivational Vision and Mission statements that say nothing, or by saying everything, communicate a message inconsistent with the business' true priorities. In this book when we refer to a business Vision or Mission we are talking about a summary of business decisions made through a Stage One or Stage Two strategic decision making process. A Vision is not meant to be an all-inclusive warm and fuzzy document. A Vision is meant to provide direction and leadership as a result of a comprehensive decision-making process.

Another company produced the following Vision as a result of a two-day management team-building exercise. The Vision read:

- ◈ We value the lasting relationships and trust we build with our clients.

- ◈ We strive at all times to demonstrate honesty and integrity.

- ◈ We see ourselves as innovative in the tools and methods we use.

> A Vision is not meant to be an all-inclusive warm and fuzzy document.

- We have a competitive drive and a high degree of determination.
- We treat our people with respect and provide extensive training.
- We want to grow the company at a sustainable pace.
- We make above-average profit margins for our industry.
- In all aspects we are and deliver the best.

How valuable is this Vision in clarifying priorities? Not very; basically this company wants to have it all (don't we all?). However, the cost of having an all-inclusive "we are the best and do everything better" Vision is that it clarifies no priorities and may set unrealistic expectations. A manager or employee in this company could justify just about any expenditure (as long as it is *honest*) as a way to further this Vision.

Many companies have Vision and Mission statements that are not the result of a strategic decision-making process. They are more often the result of

- management team brainstorming session.
- team building exercise.
- word-smithing exercise.
- marketing campaign.

None of the above activities are inherently bad; in fact they can all add value. But don't confuse these activities with the tools for defining a true business Vision. A business Vision is a visual description of what your business will look like five to ten years from now if you consistently invest in a few well defined characteristics, which together create a well-founded business strategy.

> A business Vision is a visual description of what your business will look like five to ten years from now if you consistently invest in a few well defined characteristics, which together create a well-founded business strategy.

Why Business Leaders Engage in Strategic Decision-Making

Since 1984 our mission at Applied Business Solutions, Inc. has been to provide business leaders with a comprehensive method for creating, strengthening, and maintaining a competitive advantage.

Our proven strategic decision-making process is available through retreats and seminars, books and workbooks, facilitator development, customized consulting, and public speaking presentations. The three most common ways that business leaders have profited by using our strategic decision-making tools are:

1. Developing a new business strategy and its resulting Vision.

2. Verifying or confirming a Vision and developing the confidence and goals to implement it.

3. Establishing "believe in" in your Vision by others.

Developing a New Business Strategy and Its Resulting Vision

The strategic decision-making tools presented in this book are valuable in helping you see new opportunities for yourself *and* your business. It is not unusual for a business leader to be underway without a clear Vision or specific direction to take the business. This sometimes happens when the business has reached a certain plateau, or its leader is unsure how to respond to major changes in the market. Even more common is when the business leader isn't aware of the choices, or feels like the choices are limited.

Creating a business Vision requires you know your choices *before* you choose. Choosing a direction to lead your business before you appreciate all of your choices, limits your ability to find the best solution. The critical first step in any successful strategic decision-making process is identifying your Strategic Choices. The more choices you are aware of, the better decisions you can make. Unfortunately, most people choose by selecting from a limited set of choices. We continue to be amazed at the number of business owners who have told us they felt like they had little choice about where their business was going.

For example, the owner of a computer networking service feels like he either has to grow and hire more employees or stay small and provide all the services himself. A multi-state construction firm feels like they have to go after national contracts or operate each division independently. A manufacturer has a

Choosing a direction to lead your business, before you appreciate all of your choices limits your ability to find the best solution.

single customer that orders 90 percent of his product and who wants to increase the order well past the manufacturer's present production capabilities. If the manufacturer says no he stands to lose the account, if he says yes he is taking a bigger risk by increasing his dependence on one customer.

These either/or situations are not uncommon. Perceiving only two options is a dilemma — not a choice. Strategic decision-making tools help you generate a multitude of potentially viable Strategic Choices for your business, no matter what your industry. When we work with our clients, we insist they identify and consider a minimum of nine viable Strategic Choices before making and prioritizing their final selection. If you have engaged in a business planning process that did not reveal a variety of choices for your business, then you did not participate in comprehensive strategic decision-making.

Strategic decision-making will either validate your dream and transform it into a realistic business Vision or disprove it and save you an enormous amount of time, energy, and money.

Verifying or Confirming a Vision and Developing the Confidence and Goals to Implement It

We all have dreams. Sitting and listening to another entrepreneur, you say to yourself, I could do that. Running down by the lake on Saturday morning you reflect, wouldn't it be great if we did this. Meeting annually with your partners, you agree maybe you should tackle a specific market. Daydreaming one morning you have a sudden inspiration for a new product.

It is important to understand the distinctions between a dream and a Vision because the consequences of implementing an idea that has not been properly researched or tested against market realities can be disastrous. Business leaders intuitively know this, and their resulting lack of confidence often ends up in what is known as "implementation paralysis." Even business leaders that *do* think strategically need a process that allows them to consider big picture initiatives from several perspectives. Strategic decision-making will either validate your dream and transform it into a realistic business Vision or disprove it and save you an enormous amount of time, energy, and money. The key differences between a dream and a business Vision are clarity, confidence, and viability.

◈ *Clarity.* Comes from holding your ideas up to the light of day, examining, refining, polishing, and focusing them, until they solidify into a Vision that makes good business sense.

◈ *Viability.* Is the result of decisions and choices that are researched, data-driven, and well-founded in logic.

◈ *Confidence.* Results from taking strategic decision-making through to its completion. From the formation of a business Vision to allocation of resources required to implement your annual objectives.

Without clarity of Vision, an honest assessment of viability, and the confidence that results from completing the process, you will not be prepared to implement your strategic decisions. If you do not have confidence in your decisions, no one else will.

....

Our four-stage process provides you with the tools to achieve "believe in" in your Vision from your management team, employees, and investors.

There is, of course, nothing wrong with dreams. Dreams can provide important insights into your personal goals and even be the source of undiscovered business strategies, however they are not effective tools for leading a business. Employees react negatively to lofty Vision statements that have little or no link to reality. They would prefer to get the real leadership a strategic decision-making process provides, and clear communication concerning priorities.

Your strategy and its resulting Vision and Mission should be the culmination of a comprehensive, data-driven strategic decision-making process that takes advantage of your hard earned business experience and also looks forward into the future. A process that not only builds on your Core Capabilities, but takes into account where the market is going, what the competition is doing, and how best to fulfill the business leader's Personal Definition of Success (PDS).

Establishing "Believe In" in Your Vision by Others

One of the great challenges a business owner faces is translating or transferring his Vision to others. Many business leaders have expressed their frustration at not being able to get others to listen to and understand their Vision. Our four-stage process provides you with the tools to achieve "believe in" in your Vision from your management team, employees, and investors. Having a Vision is one thing, getting other people to believe in it and act on it consistently is another.

Strategic decision-making is not only a planning tool, it is a very important communication tool. Involving others in your strategic decision-making process is an excellent way to build employee "believe-in" in your Vision. Whom to involve will depend on the stage of the process, the size of your company, and your management style. We suggest all business partners be involved in making strategic business decisions and that you expand the size of the staff you include when setting goals and objectives. When in doubt about whom to involve, we suggest you err on the side of including more people rather than fewer. Involvement in the decision-making process will increase your employees' and partners' ownership of the strategic plan, and reduce confusion when it is time to communicate and implement decisions.

Leaving a "trail of bread crumbs" that others on your team can follow is one of the key benefits of the strategic decision-making process. This is accomplished by breaking the visioning process down into manageable steps and documenting the logic and assumptions used during decision-making so that others can follow along and reach the same conclusions. Bringing your team fully aboard reduces management's tendency to micromanage and empowers your team to participate in your success at the highest possible levels.

Strategic decision-making is based on the theory and applied practice of business strategy. In the next chapter we define business strategy, explain how it shapes every business enterprise, and discuss how it can be applied to focus your business and further your success.

CHAPTER 3

Business Strategy

· ·

A group of business leaders at a national conference were asked recently, "How many of you have participated in strategic planning?" About 80 percent raised their hands. Then when asked, "How many of you *have a written strategic plan*?" about 60 percent raised their hands this time. When this same group of experienced business leaders was asked, "What is a business strategy?" the hall fell silent.

Misconceptions abound concerning business strategy. It is not unusual for a business to have a "strategic plan" that has no strategy. A business leader is better off having a business strategy with no clearly defined implementation plan than to have a strategic plan that is not based on a well thought-out strategy.

Business strategy is the development and utilization of specific qualities or characteristics that set your business apart from the other businesses within your industry. Your business strategy defines your position in the marketplace and distinguishes you from your competition. It determines your market identity, reflects the core

· · · · · · · · · · · · · · · ·

Your business strategy defines your position in the marketplace and distinguishes you from your competition.

values of your business, and drives what actions you must take to maintain and support your competitive advantage.

Your business strategy results from a comprehensive decision-making process. We call it strategic decision-making to emphasize the importance of actually making decisions that result in the development and implementation of a clear business strategy.

A business strategy will do three things for your company. It will

1. define your competitive advantage;
2. narrow who you compete with; and
3. leverage your core purpose for being in business.

Defining Your Competitive Advantage

....

How do you manage your business in order to distinguish it from the competition?

Your competitive advantage is the reason why a customer chooses your products and services over your competitors. What makes your business different from the competition? Why would a customer choose to use your product or service over someone else's? How do you manage your business in order to distinguish it from the competition? These are some of the most challenging questions business leaders will ever need to answer. The answers to these questions lead to a clearly defined competitive advantage.

A competitive advantage is gained by identifying and investing in a few specific characteristics and capabilities that distinguish you from the other businesses in your industry who provide similar products or services. The process of figuring out *which characteristics* will most effectively provide your business with a competitive advantage is the central decision in Stage One of our strategic decision-making process.

Businesses differentiate themselves in many different ways. For example, some businesses are known for:

◆ producing the highest quality product/service (Quality).

 ◈ producing the lowest cost products/service (Price).

 ◈ the most responsive delivery mechanisms (Speed).

> The number one rule of business strategy is: you cannot be all things to all people.

The number one rule of business strategy is: *you cannot be all things to all people*. A business owner cannot operationalize (put into action) the highest quality at the lowest cost while providing the shortest response time without eventually going out of business. When push comes to shove (and it does every day for business leaders) one or two of those three strategies will rise to the top and the others will be compromised. To maximize company resources and maintain a consistently recognizable market identity it is essential for a business to develop a strategy that is then used to guide all subsequent day-to-day decisions.

The triangle in Figure 3.1 represents a fairly simplistic model of business strategy. It is used to demonstrate the dynamics between the three most common characteristics that businesses use to differentiate themselves and thus attract customers. Each of the three characteristics can be developed into a competitive advantage. Combining two of the three characteristics can result in a business strategy. One of the accepted truths of this model is that a business can offer one or two but not all three triangle points at the same time.

FIGURE 3.1: Simple Business Strategy Model

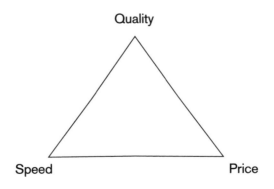

This simple model demonstrates the interaction between three distinct business strategies, each with its own costs and benefits, and each with the potential for attracting customers in a particular market. You could position your business to be:

- fast and inexpensive but quality will suffer.
- inexpensive and high quality but customers may have to wait for service.
- high quality and fast but it will be expensive.

An example of this, from the customer's point of view, was when our computer network needed some maintenance. We called three different computer support companies. The first one offered us a four-hour response time and a low hourly rate, however, they do not guarantee their work. The second one offered a guarantee on their work and a low hourly rate but they could not commit to be available on an "as needed" basis. The last option we explored was the most expensive. They offered a guarantee on their work and a commitment to find a solution within 24 hours.

There are customers in need of computer support that will be attracted to each one of the strategies used by the companies mentioned above. There is always a customer who is willing to purchase the least expensive option. There is always a customer who is willing to pay more for the best. There are always customers willing to sacrifice either price or quality in order to get the service immediately.

The purpose behind strategic decision-making is to position your business, choose the "right" customers and prospects, and manage your operational (day-to-day) decisions consistent with your strategy.

A small toy manufacturer was thrilled when their specialty toy took off. The business owner's Vision had been to create the *best* toy possible. As demand rose they bought additional technology to speed up the manufacturing process and were forced to run the plant 24-hours-a-day. Still, they had difficulty keeping up with orders, and the toys started to leave the factory with air bubbles in them. These quality errors not only affected

The purpose behind strategic decision-making is to position your business, choose the "right" customers and prospects, and manage your operational (day-to-day) decisions consistent with your strategy.

the performance of the toy but also made the toy less visually appealing. What was the owner to do? Should they ship now while the market is hot or slow down to ensure quality doesn't suffer? Should they raise prices to compensate for the true cost of consistently high quality? If, through a comprehensive strategic decision-making process, the manufacturer had chosen quality as their competitive advantage then, in order to retain that strategic position, they must slow down production to ensure they consistently meet their high quality standards.

The strategy triangle in Figure 3.1 demonstrates the dynamics of making strategic decisions between competing characteristics, however, in the real world there are a lot more ways in which businesses can, and do, differentiate themselves. For example, not all fast-food restaurants compete directly with each other. Look at the extensive marketing campaigns of the different fast-food restaurants and you will appreciate how hard they work at distinguishing themselves. Think about all the different ways these restaurants set themselves apart from one another. They may compete through:

- quality of the food
- quantity of food
- price of food
- speed of service
- friendliness of staff
- drive-through capability
- convenience of location
- clean restrooms and other amenities
- standardization of the menu and the product
- offering specialty foods
- offering delivery services
- inclusion of family fun equipment and children's meals

Highly successful companies have combined several unique characteristics and capabilities together to form strategies that really set them apart. They then consistently invest in those strategies to develop a strong competitive advantage and resulting market position. The following companies exemplify businesses that have identified a clear strategy and leveraged it into a competitive advantage.

- ◈ Amazon.com put themselves on the map by combining e-commerce, excellent distribution, and competitive pricing to sell commodity products including books, music, and art.

- ◈ Starbucks created a brand and a completely new niche in the coffee industry. They created a worldwide network of company-owned coffee shops, specialty coffee drinks, and retail products.

- ◈ America Online established itself as the standard of Internet Service Providers by offering a worldwide network of access numbers, dominating the market by purchasing their biggest competitor (CompuServe), and offering exclusive membership services and advertising opportunities.

- ◈ Southwest Airlines set itself apart in the airline industry by providing budget prices, minimal services, and quick turnaround on secondary routes.

Take a moment to explore how your business distinguishes itself from others within your industry. What is your competitive advantage? Use Worksheet 3 to help you better understand your current business strategy.

The tighter the focus you have on the priorities established by your business strategy, the more clear and successful that strategy becomes.

> The tighter the focus you have on the priorities established by your business strategy, the more clear and successful that strategy becomes.

Narrowing the Competition

Business strategy divides businesses from the same industry into separate competitive arenas. Your strategy narrows the number of businesses you compete with. One of the benefits of

WORKSHEET 3: How Clearly Defined Is Your Business Strategy?

Your competitive advantage is the result of carefully selecting and prioritizing the characteristics and capabilities that set you apart and differentiate your business from the competition. Use this simple assessment tool to identify what differentiates your business from the competition today. Score the importance of the following attributes in your ability to attract and retain customers. Circle how effectively you compete on each of the following characteristics using a scale of one to five (five being highest).

1.	The consistency of your product line.	1	2	3	4	5
2.	Your ability to develop products or services to solve your client's problems.	1	2	3	4	5
3.	Your capability to get your product/service to your customers.	1	2	3	4	5
4.	Your commitment to hiring and retaining qualified personnel.	1	2	3	4	5
5.	The superior quality of your product line.	1	2	3	4	5
6.	The low cost of your product line.	1	2	3	4	5
7.	The breadth of your product line.	1	2	3	4	5
8.	Application of technology in producing or selling your product line.	1	2	3	4	5
9.	The brand, size, or market dominance of your company.	1	2	3	4	5
10.	The way you find and develop sales with potential customers.	1	2	3	4	5

KEY:

If you scored a 5 in one, two, or three places then you may have a clear strategy in place.

If you scored a 5 in four or more places then you may not have a clear strategy.

If you scored a 5 in more than six places then you most likely have no clear strategy at all.

A high score in this assessment test indicates that you have not clearly set your strategic priorities.

developing a business strategy is that you can choose which businesses you will compete with.

Has anyone ever said to you, "I'm thinking about buying a new car and I can't decide whether to get a Lexus ES 300 or a Hyundai Sonata?" Probably not; both Lexus and Hyundai are in the same industry (car manufacturing), but they do not compete directly for the same customers. Lexus' competitive advantage (the reason people buy their cars) is they design and build high end, maintenance free, status-enhancing cars. Hyundai's competitive advantage is they offer entry level, economical, and practical transportation. Neither strategy is inherently better than the other; there are customers for both. Both Lexus and Hyundai are managed as profitable and distinct business entities.

A hardwood floor installer saw that the vast majority of the industry advertised themselves as experts in high quality custom installation. He recognized this as an opportunity to capture the attention of price-conscious customers by being the lowest cost provider and by developing do-it-yourself kits. As a result he is no longer directly in competition with high-end custom floor installers. He has created a new market niche, which includes the development of a different set of products, and a focus on an under-served market: the homeowner, hobbyist, and budget-conscious contractor.

Automobile dealerships, who generate a large part of their revenue by servicing vehicles they have sold, do not compete directly with oil-change shops like the Grease Monkey. A travel agency offering experience in high-end international leisure travel does not compete with e-ticketing agencies. Every company has its own set of competitors, based on their business strategy, and as a result each attracts a different set of customers.

When you do not have a clearly defined business strategy it is very difficult to narrow whom you compete with. For example, many professional service firms are managed inconsistently with little or no concrete strategy. They may have an area of expertise but they are willing to provide services outside that

> One of the benefits of developing a business strategy is that you can choose which businesses you will compete with.

area of expertise when asked to do so. They may have quality ideals but they have no systems to monitor the quality of their performance.

In a recent search for an intellectual property attorney we interviewed several law firms. When we asked one firm who their target market is they replied, "Well everybody! Who eventually doesn't need an attorney?" Companies without a clear business strategy pay a high price for competing with everybody. They have no consistent message or tools for qualifying clients or prospects, they are unable to successfully structure strategic alliances with others within their industry, and they have no clear framework to use for focused, targeted, marketing. These "we can do anything for most anybody" companies find they compete with everyone in their respective industries.

When first starting business consulting, we would attend professional associations, and everyone was a potential competitor. We couldn't imagine what the value of networking would be within the industry. As far as we were concerned we were fraternizing with the enemy! However, once we had a clear business strategy in hand, consultants that were previously perceived as competition now began to look more like referral sources, possible strategic alliances, and even customers.

With no clear competitive advantage you feel like you are competing with the world. Clearly defining your market position helps you to identify and target customers attracted to your unique combination of characteristics and capabilities. This appreciation elevates you above others in your industry and helps you clearly identify whom you are competing with. One of the benefits of identifying a clear business strategy is that you limit your direct competition and as a result you are in a better position to win.

> One of the benefits of identifying a clear business strategy is that you limit your direct competition and as a result you are in a better position to win.

Leveraging Your Core Purpose for Being in Business

The way business is conducted has changed dramatically over the last ten years. More than ever people are striving to create a lasting legacy. Business leaders are no longer interested in leaving their personal values and goals at home when they go to work. Everyone wants to find a way to make a lasting positive contribution while at the same time making a living. Those contributions can take many forms, such as:

- labor relations
- business ethics
- product benefits
- environmental/social impact
- personal lifestyle choices

....

What are the enduring contributions that you, through your business, want to leave the world as a legacy?

One of the realities of small business is that a few people, the owner, partners, or principals, have a huge impact on the success of the business and the direction in which it moves. What are the enduring contributions that you, through your business, want to leave the world as a legacy? What is the larger purpose for your being in business? What does your business stand for besides manufacturing gadgets and making money?

Not only is it possible to incorporate your personal values and passions into your business life so as to make your workday more satisfying and fulfilling, but you can also turn them into a competitive advantage by including them in your business strategy. After all, if you are looking for a unique ingredient to help set your company apart, what could be more unique than your personal strengths, interests, and values? What is the greater good you are committed to achieving? Providing long-term secure employment for the families in your community? Keeping children off drugs, saving lives in developing countries, expanding access to transportation for all, making homes safer and more loving environments for children? These are but a few of the ways you can make a positive impact with your business while at the same time strengthening your competitive advantage.

Kay Harai's Studio 901, in Seattle, created a competitive advantage by leveraging her personal commitment to the use of environmentally-friendly hair care products. The owner's personal commitment to the environment is embodied in the business strategy and makes a statement many consumers are very attracted to. The result is a strategy that successfully sets Studio 901 apart from the competition.

Bill Gates, the founder of Microsoft, has a *vision* of "a paperless office." This *vision* of a better world drives many of Microsoft's product development decisions.

Patagonia's business strategy revolves around its founder, Yvon Chouinard's, passion for saving the earth's natural resources. Ten percent of their pre-tax profit is donated to grass-roots organizations involved in direct action campaigns focused on preservation and protection of the environment.

> The right course is a strategy that is fueled by the personal motivations and goals of the business leader.

One of the principles that makes this decision-making model unique is our commitment to helping business leaders reveal the right course for themselves, as well as for their business. The right course is a strategy that is fueled by the personal motivations and goals of the business leader. These goals are then balanced with the requirements and needs of the marketplace. The most successful (business) people are those who are doing work they love, something that is meaningful to them.

A good business Vision is more than just the sum of its parts. It is the target that you aim for, the values that are meaningful to both the owners and employees, and the principles with which you motivate your entire team. Your business is more than simply a conduit for money to pass through. What a business stands for reflects the values of its leader(s), and the value it provides to the world at large through the products and services it offers. These values contribute powerfully to the substance of a well-developed business strategy.

A solid strategy can provide your business with a clear and compelling competitive advantage. It also narrows the number of businesses with whom you directly compete, and it creates forward momentum by drawing on the powers inherent in your core purpose for being in business. How do you create a comprehensive strategy for your business? The answer is: strategic decision-making.

The Strategic Plan

Your strategic plan records the strategy you have chosen as a result of completing a comprehensive strategic decision-making process.

Your strategic plan clearly states the direction you have chosen to take your business. It describes the characteristics you have chosen to leverage into a competitive advantage. It lays out the goal areas you will address over the next five to ten years, and the specific objectives you will work to achieve over the next 12 months to realize your goals. The plan also includes a realistic budget to support the implementation of your goals and objectives.

Your strategic plan records the strategy you have chosen as a result of completing a comprehensive strategic decision-making process. It clearly outlines the decisions you made in each of the four stages. Your strategic plan should include:

- ◆ Your business strategy.
- ◆ A list of the different Strategic Choices you have considered.
- ◆ A data-driven Market Forecast.

♦ A Competitive Analysis.

♦ The business owner's Personal Definition of Success.

♦ The business' Core Capabilities.

♦ The top four prioritized Strategic Choices that form the basis of your vision.

♦ The characteristics and capabilities that make your business unique and that form your competitive advantage.

♦ The Vision for your business five to ten years from now.

♦ Your competitive advantage, and the actions you must take to develop, leverage, and maintain it.

♦ Your target market.

♦ A prioritized list of the products and services you have chosen to offer.

♦ Your business Mission.

♦ A survey of your business' current position.

♦ Five to seven business goal areas.

♦ Annual objectives with the resources allocated to achieve those objectives in the next 12 months.

Your strategic plan is an internal document that is designed to record and communicate your company's competitive advantage, target market, long-term goals, and business objectives to your management team and employees. It creates a context for making all subsequent operational decisions. It is a record of the decisions made, and the logic and assumptions that led up to those decisions. It is also a business management tool used to track and reward progress toward your Vision.

How long it takes to fully implement a strategy and achieve the Vision you are aiming toward is dependent on two variables. The first is how big of a course change you will be making as a result of your strategic decision-making. The second is the amount of resources you have available to support your goals and objectives. Although you can choose a longer, and in some rare cases a shorter timeframe for your strategic plan, we

....

Your strategic plan is basically an internal document that is designed to record and communicate your company's competitive advantage, target market, long-term goals, and business objectives to your management team and employees.

A plan that
encompasses more than
ten years is often too
long because there is a
tendency to lose sight of
your Vision.

recommend a five to ten year time span. Five years is generally the minimum amount of time it takes to affect significant and consistent change in the way you do business. A plan that encompasses more than ten years is often too long because there is a tendency to lose sight of your Vision. The amount of time it actually takes to fully implement a strategy becomes clearer as you define five-year goals and the objectives that support them.

A strategic plan is:

- A foundation for a business plan.

- A tool for communicating company priorities.

- A management process that is used on an annual or quarterly basis to adjust, when needed, the direction of the business.

- Your strategic plan includes the integration of the budget and management's operational expectations.

Foundation for a Business Plan

A strategic plan has a different purpose than a business plan. A business plan is primarily a tool designed to project the viability of financial investments and solicit investment capital. The main decisions from a strategic plan are often presented in the introduction to a business plan. However, a business plan does not necessarily require a comprehensive strategic decision-making process.

A client of ours hired an accounting firm to help her write a business plan to secure bank financing for purchasing a large piece of equipment. She is the owner of a mid-sized construction company and is always keeping an eye out for equipment bargains. A huge crane came on the market after being custom-designed and only partially completed. She considered it a bargain because she has the equipment maintenance staff and facilities that could finish the crane, and she could purchase this huge piece of equipment at far below the cost of having one built for her firm.

The CPA firm was able to project the financial requirements for purchasing this large piece of equipment and together they created a business plan that the bank then used to approve the loan. Before she knew it, our client was the proud owner of a big, yellow crane.

It was a year later that we started working with this client. The crane still stood in the yard needing to be completed. They had used it during the holidays for a very impressive Christmas light display, but had not yet allocated the resources to get it finished. We weren't long into the strategic decision-making process before it became obvious that the work the crane was designed to do, may in fact not be the right work for the firm to do.

The business leader was struck with the realization, that if she were to choose the direction she really wanted to take the firm, she did not need the crane. Her other choice was to be driven by the opportunity she had already invested in — the crane. Luckily for this business leader she had a choice. Many business leaders are not so fortunate. They grab onto opportunities that subsequently begin driving the business and have a difficult time regaining control.

A business plan is a tool to clarify if you can. A strategic plan is a tool to clarify if you should.

Just Because You Can, Does Not Mean You Should

If the first tenet of strategic decision-making is *you can't be everything to everybody* then the second tenet of strategic decision-making is, *just because you can, does not mean you should.* A business plan is a tool to clarify *if you can.* A strategic plan is a tool to *clarify if you should* — and if the answer is yes, then what is the best way to go about it. Using just a business plan, that is not backed up by a well thought-out strategic plan, may lead you down a path that doesn't go where you expect it. The business plan uses financial models to calculate if it is financially feasible for you to make a specific investment. However, just because it is financially *feasible* does not make it a good idea.

Many business owners purchase equipment, sign leases, hire staff, or make any number of large investments that add little value, and consume irreplaceable resources, because they did not first subject the opportunity to comprehensive scrutiny. The strategic plan is the foundation for a business plan. The business plan itself is, generally speaking, an external document used simply to evaluate the viability of a business prior to making a capital investment.

A Tool for Communicating Company Priorities

We recently completed a strategic decision-making retreat for a regional dental clinic. During Stage Four, the setting of objectives, which includes employee feedback and participation, the owner made an astute observation. He told his team that as long as everyone "was paddling in the same direction" it would be an improvement, even if they were going a little off-course. We heartily agree with him as to the impossible-to-underestimate value of having everyone on your team paddling in the same direction.

....

Your business is a vessel for achieving your Vision.

Your business is a vessel for achieving your Vision. Like a vessel it is underway, and each employee is part of your locomotion. If your employees do not know what your strategic priorities are, how can they make decisions consistent with your strategy? Every day, every one of your employees, from the mail clerk to the president, makes decisions that either are or are not consistent with your business strategy. Decisions that are made inconsistently with your Vision often lead to lost productivity, loss of market share, and a confusing market identity.

Remember the toy manufacturer in Chapter 2, the one who chose to make the highest quality toy? As demand for the toy increased, they increased production. An assembly worker was among the first to notice small defects appearing. He remembered reading something about the company strategy that said it is a higher priority to maintain high quality toys than to produce large quantities of toys. So he reported the defects to the production manager. The production manager, who had participated in the strategic decision-making process, immediately realized that a potentially big problem had arisen. He checked in with the shipping clerk, who showed him a small pile of the toys he had put aside because he too was aware of the company's strategy. He brought the matter to the attention of the management team for further consideration. The management team then had the choice of staying on course and taking operational actions to address the quality issues, or taking a different course and being prepared for how that change would affect their market position and identity.

The strategic plan also serves as a communication tool simply by getting your Vision *out of your head and onto paper*. Again, how can your team help you achieve your Vision if they don't know what it is? Getting it out on paper gives you, and whatever advisers you choose to include, a chance to validate or disprove your ideas before the costly process of operationalizing begins. Having your facts, assumptions, and decisions on paper makes them easier to check and communicate.

Declaring who you are and what your business stands for is another use of the strategic plan as a communication tool. Your Mission statement, the part of your strategic plan that is used externally as well as internally, communicates who your target market is, what your priority products or services are, and how you provide those products or services that distinguish you from your competitors. It is a public statement that is designed to attract your target market by having them recognize themselves and their needs, as well as the benefits of coming to your company to fill those needs.

A strategic plan is a tool for communicating what your priorities are. Your team is then much more able and willing to support your Vision, and your customers and prospects have little doubt over who you are and the advantages of purchasing services from you.

A Management Process

Your strategic plan is the foundation for the strategic management of your company. Strategic management simply put, is making all your day-to-day decisions consistent with a single over-riding principle, your strategy.

Declaring who you are and what your business stands for is another use of the strategic plan as a communication tool.

A strategic plan, however, is not a guarantee of perpetual success. Developing a strategy based on the four key perspectives, and thereafter making operational decisions consistent with that strategy, will move you light-years ahead of the competition. But just like the rest of life, there are no absolutes when it comes to business strategy.

By definition if one company comes up with a great strategy, it will only work for them as long as they are one of the few businesses in their industry using that strategy or they continue to operationalize it better than anyone else. For example, Amazon.com was the first company to really take advantage of selling books over the Internet. They used the Internet as a unique method of sales that enabled them to compete on price and convenience with traditional brick and mortar booksellers. But when Barnes & Noble adopted a similar Internet strategy, online customers all of a sudden had a choice, and Amazon.com started to lose their competitive advantage. The two giant booksellers then had to refine their strategies and find new ways to differentiate themselves in order to gain and maintain market share.

> Your strategic plan is a living, breathing, evolving document that must be used and updated to provide its fullest benefits.

How often should you review your strategic plan? Your strategic plan is a living, breathing, evolving document that must be used and updated to provide its fullest benefits. Check your plan as follows:

- Ongoing as a guide to your operational decisions.
- Quarterly (minimum) to check on progress toward goals and objectives.
- Annually to make sure that the assumptions and logic that led up to the formation of your strategy still hold true, and to set new, annual business objectives.

Following up on your strategic plan is a way to hold your team accountable for achieving their objectives. It is also a tool they can use to hold *you* accountable.

When you complete a strategic decision-making process, you can anticipate that those members of your team not immediately involved in the process will be tentative in their support of the plan. How many times has your business begun an operational initiative and not followed through? How many times have you asked your team to be "all things to all customers?" Learning to use a strategic plan as a strategic management tool takes discipline and follow through. It is not until the business leader and management team consistently follow through and use the plan that the rest of the team will do likewise.

> Learning to use a strategic plan as a strategic management tool takes discipline and follow through.

To get the most out of it, treat your plan as though it is alive. Update it, revisit it often, and use it for each and every major decision. One of our clients, Jim Larkin of Romac Industries, has been utilizing our strategic decision-making model for the last eight years. He reports that "using a well defined business strategy feels very natural, reduces the amount of time it takes to make good decisions, increases everyone's confidence, and facilitates the delegation of decision-making to the lowest level in the organization possible." The bottom line is it makes his job easier and enhances the success of the company.

Integration of the Budget and Management's Operational Expectations

Your strategic plan is used to define operational expectations and annual objectives for your company. With your priorities clearly in mind and a solid vision of the future, you will want to integrate your strategic plan into your budgeting and performance management process.

A community mortgage bank wants to sustain its growth long after the refinance boom is over. Their strategic plan revolves around strengthening their expertise with multi-family housing and building lasting relationships with developers. All their loan brokers understood and agreed with the plan, but because it is easier to refinance a single family home, that is how the brokers continued to invest their time. The brokers' incentive was based solely on the *volume* of loans they brought in, not the *type* of loans they originated. It was not until the leaders of the bank looked at their incentive systems that they saw the inconsistency between their business strategy and their performance management systems.

Having a business strategy that is not supported by your internal business management processes will hinder progress toward your Vision. In this case the bank had not integrated their pay structure for brokers into their business strategy. There was no incentive for the broker to go after the harder-to-find loan origination in the multi-family market. Once the bank revamped their incentive system in support of their business strategy, they started to pick up the speed and momentum they needed to be repositioned before the refinance market cooled.

Annual budgets and performance expectations are an integral part of your strategic plan. You will want to ensure your chart of accounts, your incentive systems, your job descriptions, and your management structure all support the business strategy. Each of these management tools can be designed to support a particular business strategy. If they are still designed to support the strategy your father was using when he opened the business 30 years ago, then your management systems are, in fact, working against you today.

It is wise to remember that a strategic plan is not:

- A wish list or unrealistic dream.
- A team-building exercise.
- A set of goals based on a quick decision.
- A secretive document to be kept from others' view.
- A guarantee of a successful business.
- A career-planning process.
- The result of a brainstorming session.

Having a business strategy that is not supported by your internal business management processes will hinder progress toward your Vision.

Further Benefits of Having a Strategic Plan Are

- It makes your job easier.
- It helps maximize the Return-on-Investment of your resources.

Making Your Job Easier

Having a clearly defined strategic plan makes your job easier. Your strategic plan provides the foundation for day-to-day decision-making. The decisions that constitute your strategic plan form the foundation for making all ongoing operational decisions with consistency and ease.

Your completed plan provides the easily referenced decision-making criteria you keep by your and the management team's desks. It lays out your long- and short-term priorities, providing a context for making day-to-day decisions. Your operational decisions are made in alignment and support of your chosen strategy. If they are not, you often wind up squandering time, energy, and money.

The leader of a regional travel agency has developed a strategy that includes staffing major corporate accounts with a travel agent at the client's location to handle all their business travel requirements. A friend calls and tells her about a fabulous new retail location opening up in an upscale urban mall. She considers the opportunity for a minute, knowing that she doesn't have many competitors in that area and that the retail space would be an excellent location for a leisure-travel agency. She asks herself, "How would expanding into this location support our strategy? Would it appeal to my target market?" The answer is no, it would not. Opening that other location would be like opening another business entirely and would divert needed resources from the successful niche she worked hard to carve out.

Another trusted business adviser recommends she invest in an e-ticketing reservation system. Again she reflects, "How will e-ticketing help us better serve and retain our competitive position and our target market?" By looking at these opportunities in the larger context of her strategy, she is able to quickly decide whether to just let them go or give them further consideration.

One of the great benefits that business leaders love about their strategic plans is the assignment of accountability to specific people within their organizations to accomplish specific goals and objectives by specific dates. In other words: *who* is responsible to accomplish *what* by *when*. A key factor here is writing objectives

Your strategic plan provides the foundation for day-to-day decision-making.

that are result vs. process-oriented and SMART (Specific, Measurable, Agreed-upon, Realistic, with a Tracking system). Completing your strategic decision-making and recording it in a comprehensive plan will make your job easier.

Maximizing the Return on Investment of Your Resources

Planning is proven to be more cost-effective and provides a higher return-on-investment than working without a plan. Whether designing a new product, launching a new market campaign, providing a service, or writing a customer letter, each act is more effectively achieved, in less time, when carefully planned before beginning. Most companies cannot afford to waste money, raw material, space, expertise, and human resources on unfocused activity. Businesses come to us that have hired marketing people but who have not yet defined their target markets. Others have launched new products before defining their key product areas. Still others have hired management-training firms but have not defined the priorities they want to instill in their people. It may feel more productive to put ideas into action than it does to decide where you are headed. However, all you are gaining is the illusion of momentum. Movement without clearly defined direction rarely results in significant progress toward the long-term success of your company. Time spent planning will always save time, dollars, and frustration later.

> It may feel more productive to put ideas into action than it does to decide where you are headed. However, all you are gaining is the illusion of momentum.

You can rely on luck and the vagaries of the winds to be successful, or you can systematically navigate your company toward your preferred destination. A well thought-out plan is far more efficient than a random course. Planning requires some investment of management time, focus, and commitment. These resources are often in short supply, but it is not half as expensive to invest management time in planning, as it is to just start doing, and risk moving in the wrong direction. Use Worksheet 4 to review your business experiences with doing and planning.

Chapters 5 through 10 detail the strategic decision-making process, the result of which is a viable and compelling strategic plan.

WORKSHEET 4: The Cost of Doing Before Planning

A. List three examples of projects or business directions you launched without a clear plan. What were the consequences of doing without planning?

Project	Consequences
Example: Printing a brochure that did not reach your target market.	Wasted $65,000
1.	
2.	
3.	

B. List three examples of projects that were launched with a clearly thought-out plan. What were the consequences of investing time in planning before launching the project?

Project	Consequences
Example: Use market research to focus telemarketing efforts.	28% close rate
1.	
2.	
3.	

Strategic Choices

Business strategy is the development and utilization of specific qualities or characteristics that set your business apart from the other businesses within your industry. Understanding all the options available to you and your business, before you choose a strategy, is critical to the success of the strategic decision-making process. This chapter focuses on generating Strategic Choices, the potential characteristics, capabilities, or opportunities that can be used to distinguish your business and give it a competitive edge. Identifying Strategic Choices is the first step in Stage One of the strategic decision-making process.

Strategic Choices are the building blocks of a business strategy.

Strategic Choices are the building blocks of business strategy. Each Strategic Choice represents a different way that your business could distinguish itself and a different direction you could take your business to achieve a particular Vision. You might, at first glance, think of a Strategic Choice as actually being a strategy all by itself. But a single Strategic Choice cannot stand alone as a comprehensive business strategy. It must be combined and prioritized with other Strategic Choices in order to create a viable business strategy, and its related Vision, for your business.

Strategic Choices for a florist could include:

- Creating an alliance with hospitals as a method of selling flowers.

- Focusing on their expertise in orchids and tropical flowers.

- Becoming part of a national floral distribution network like FTD.

- Offering flower packages where bouquets are sent to a residence regularly on a pre-arranged schedule.

- Positioning the shop on the busiest corner in town.

- Offering classes in floral design.

- Offering flower arrangements for the caterers in the region.

- Developing a franchise concept and selling it to other florists.

Each of these ideas could potentially set this florist shop apart from its competition. Combining and prioritizing several of these Strategic Choices, and investing in them consistently, results in a business strategy.

Transforming an Opportunity Into a Strategic Choice

Understanding the intention behind a specific opportunity is key to developing Strategic Choices.

To develop a particular capability or opportunity into a Strategic Choice, you align it with a specific *differentiator*, thus clarifying on what basis you will use that capability to compete. In this next section you will learn how to transform opportunities into realistic Strategic Choices for your business by exploring the nine basic ways that all businesses use to differentiate and distinguish themselves.

Opportunity + Differentiator = Strategic Choice

Understanding the intention behind a specific opportunity is key to developing Strategic Choices. Remember our friend Bob Inkman from Chapter 1? One of the several opportunities he is faced with is to invest in technology, perhaps by updating his printing capabilities through the purchase of a digital printing press. This is an expensive option so it is important for Bob to be clear and confident in his decision. Why should he buy a new technologically advanced press? What is the motivation behind his consideration of this opportunity?

- Is he considering the purchase of this new equipment because it will enable him to better meet the various needs of a specific type of customer? If so, the motivation behind this opportunity is to position his shop as the preferred provider of printing services to a specific market.

- Is he considering the purchase of this new equipment because it will enable him to print faster and cheaper than his competitors? If so, then the motivation behind this opportunity is to position his shop to be more production efficient.

- Is he considering the purchase of this new equipment because it will enable him to produce higher quality, four-color, long run printing than anyone in his region? If so, the motivation behind this opportunity is to position his shop as the local expert in four-color printing.

The opportunity for Bob is to invest in a technologically advanced printing press. If he does, then the press potentially becomes a characteristic that will set him apart from his competition. It is essential however that Bob first understand the underlying motivation behind the opportunity. Why? Say that for the past ten years Bob's shop has been well known for quick printing at reasonable prices with moderate quality. If he invests in technology that produces very high quality printing and he has to raise prices to accommodate the expense, then he will be shifting his market position. He might lose his old customers because they are accustomed to lower prices, and he will have to initiate a new marketing program, with its associated costs, to attract customers that are looking for the new service he offers. He also may unknowingly put himself in direct competition with several other local businesses that can match his quality at a lesser cost. It is essential that Bob understand the basis on which he has chosen to compete, and that he makes informed decisions consistent with that basis.

Do all restaurants compete on the same basis? In Chapter 3 we listed a number of ways in which restaurants compete. Restaurants like McDonalds and Burger King compete for customers who want fast, inexpensive, consistently recognizable food. Restaurants like McCormick & Schmicks and Ruth Chris' Steak House in downtown Seattle compete for the business luncheon and dinner crowd. But does McDonalds compete for the same business as Ruth Chris' Steak House? No, these restaurants compete using different differentiators. They are not in direct competition for the same customers. Some restaurants compete on the basis of price, some on location, some on quality.

Within any given industry, not all businesses compete directly. In fact, there are nine basic ways that a business can combine and use to create a competitive advantage. We call these nine basic ways, differentiators because they embody the crucial characteristics that differentiate your business from the competition.

> There are basically nine different ways that a business can create a competitive advantage.

Transforming a Differentiator Into a Strategic Choice

The differentiators define on what basis businesses compete. Aligning an opportunity or capability, available to your business, with a differentiator results in a Strategic Choice. Strategic Choices are real-life applications of the differentiators to your business. They clarify the motivation behind the particular opportunities you are considering investing in.

Differentiator + Opportunity = Strategic Choice

Assume three other print shops in Bob's town do what Bob does at similar prices. These shops compete on a pretty similar basis, and there is very little differentiation between them. Bob realizes that he and his competitors reach out to their customers through the same newspapers, yellow pages, radio spots, etc. and decides to find a new way of selling his services. Method of Sale is one of the nine differentiators that distinguish businesses from each other. Finding a unique method of selling your services can set you apart and be one of the characteristics of an effective business strategy.

Bob notices that booksellers, grocers, and other merchants are having success with the Internet and decides to check it out. He has a Web page and some proprietary software developed that allows customers to see what their final projects will look like, make prepress adjustments, e-mail their projects in, and pay for it all online.

> Method of Sale is one of the nine differentiators that distinguish businesses from each other.

The opportunity in this case is the use of the Internet. If the intent behind using the Internet is to sell services in a unique fashion, then the differentiator is Method of Sale. The specific way Bob intends to use the Internet as a Method of Sale (the Web page and proprietary software) is referred to as a Strategic Choice. In other words, a realistic Strategic Choice for Bob's print shop is to develop a Web page and proprietary software that enables his customers to see what their final projects will look like in advance, make prepress adjustments, e-mail their projects in, and pay for it all online. The difference between this example and the previous one (concerning the printing press), is that in this case Bob started by first identifying a differentiator and then found a unique way to utilize it. In the first example, Bob started with a pre-existing opportunity and discovered the differentiator behind it.

Differentiator (Method of Sale) + Opportunity (Internet) =
Strategic Choice (Web Page and Software)

Every action we take as business leaders requires an investment, however many of these investments do not provide the type of return we had anticipated. Often this is because we did not take the time to fully appreciate what the purpose was behind the investment. Why did Recreational Equipment Inc. (REI) build a climbing wall inside their Seattle store? Why did Nordstrom open stores across the nation? Why do car manufacturers offer factory rebates? Why does an accounting firm join forces with an engineering firm? Why do you invest your resources in the way you do?

Investing in certain opportunities just because everyone else does can only result in you staying a little behind the rest of the pack — always in a race to play catch up. Why do all rental car agencies provide unlimited mileage? Many of the more mature industries have copied themselves to such extremes that they have turned into commodities. The only way to differentiate among them is through pricing. And at that point the industry turns into what is commonly referred to as a commodity market. But for those willing to explore strategic alternatives for each of the nine differentiators there is always a new way to provide an old product or service.

The Nine Types of Differentiators

Our differentiators are based on a Driving Forces® model developed by Kepner-Tregoe. The differentiators shape your business. They define your position in the marketplace, the products and services you offer, and how you offer them. They embody the crucial characteristics that customers and prospects use to determine who they are going to select to do business with. The differentiators are used, to some degree, by all businesses to distinguish themselves from each other. The differentiators divide businesses that are in the same industry into separate competitive arenas.

We use differentiators to clarify the intention or purpose behind a specific opportunity, and to provide business leaders with a method for identifying Strategic Choices that can be combined to form a competitive advantage. Your competitive advantage, the way that customers perceive your business, is shaped and defined by the way you apply these differentiators and how much you invest proportionately in each of them. The working definitions for our differentiators follow:

· ·

Your competitive advantage, the way that customers perceive your business, is shaped and defined by the way you apply and prioritize the differentiators and how much you invest in them.

1. *Market Responsive*: Market Responsive companies have identified a specific "named" market that they are responding to. Once this market is identified, Market Responsive companies develop new products and services in response to *that specific market's needs*. These companies

are often known as generalists. Their specialty is in understanding the needs of their "named market," more than the specific products and services they provide. Once a market's needs are identified, the Market Responsive company responds by developing or providing access to those products the market is requesting. These companies are generally characterized by large, diverse, service or product offerings.

To exemplify the differentiators take a look at the hospitality industry. The hotel chain, U.S. Suites that has adopted the "extended stay" concept is a good example of how a hotel can successfully compete by being Market Responsive. The concept of extended stays was developed as a unique way to service a named market, business travelers. They provide mini-suites with small food preparation areas, as well as all the other business-related conveniences a business traveler may require. Successful companies from other industries that may use Market Responsive as one of their top differentiators include: Toys R Us, Weight Watchers, Kinkos, and Canon.

2. *Products or Services Superiority*: Product Superiority companies are specialists. As a result of their narrow product or service scope they are generally known as the best, or the experts, within their product or service area. These companies tend to specialize and strive to be the highest quality provider in a specific product or service area. Superiority-driven companies focus their efforts on increasing the quality and reputation of their limited line of products or services.

The Four Seasons Olympic in Seattle is an example of a hotel that uses Superiority as one of its top differentiators. It is a premier hotel located in a metro center offering expensive and exclusive guest experiences, and as a result they rarely compete on price. Successful companies from other industries that use Superiority as one of their top differentiators include: Rolls Royce, Applied Business Solutions, Inc., and Cathay Pacific.

> Superiority-driven companies focus their efforts on increasing the quality and reputation of their limited line of products or services.

3. *Production Efficiency*: Production Efficient companies make it a priority to keep their existing production or service delivery capabilities at full capacity and operating at maximum efficiency. These companies are positioned to provide fast turn around and very consistent, minimal customization products or services. These companies are often characterized by their ability to produce a product or service inexpensively, in large volumes, or within short timelines and to be price competitive.

Examples of hotels that use Production Efficiency as one of their top differentiators would be Econo Lodge, Motel 6, or Howard Johnsons. Successful companies from other industries that may use Production Efficiency as one of their top differentiators include: Ford, McDonalds, Anheuser-Busch, Walgreens, The Office Factory.

4. *Natural or Human Resources*: A dependence on Human or Natural Resources can be used to create a competitive advantage. The key to using a natural or human resource as a competitive advantage is control of access to that resource. Natural Resources traditionally include fossil fuels, timber, crops, destinations, and metals. However, there are many other ways to utilize this differentiator. The physical location of a business, whether downtown with high foot-traffic, or in a tax-free zone, can result in a competitive advantage.

Human resources can also be turned into a competitive advantage. If you are the only restaurant with a "named" world-renowned chef, then you have a characteristic (the chef) that sets you apart and provides you with a competitive advantage. If customers are drawn to your firm or shop specifically because of the individuals who work for you, those people can become your competitive advantage.

Hotels often use Natural Resources as a differentiator. An example is the Crater Lake Lodge in Oregon. It is the hotel's proximity to Crater Lake that gives it a competitive

The key to using a natural or human resource as a competitive advantage is control of access to that resource.

advantage. Wilbur Rumplebutt's B & B in Portland, Maine is successful because guests return specifically for Wilbur's gracious hospitality. Successful companies from other industries that may use Natural or Human Resources as one of their top differentiators include: Weyerhaeuser and the Emerald Room (atop Seattle's Space Needle). Many professional service firms that are named after their principals are Human Resource driven.

5. *Market Dominance*: Market Dominance only provides a real competitive advantage once you are the largest (or one of the largest) in your industry, or own a majority of market share in a specific market or product area. As a result, Market Dominant companies set goals to build, expand, and control market share. Once a company develops a brand name and gains a large enough percentage of the market share they are in a better position to control pricing and quality standards across the industry. These businesses constantly strive for continual and significant growth in market share and may do so through mergers, acquisitions, price-cutting, or radical investments in expansion. The competitive advantage is achieved as a result of market dominance via size and brand recognition.

Examples of hotels that may use Market Dominance as one of their top differentiators are the Holiday Inn and the Marriott. Successful companies from other industries that use Market Dominance as one of their top differentiators include: Coca-Cola, Microsoft, and Amazon.com. Note that all the nationally known companies mentioned as examples of the differentiators are competing on the basis of Market Dominance in addition to the other differentiator they are used to exemplify.

It is important to appreciate that wanting to grow your company is significantly different than using Market Dominance as a differentiator. Ask yourself: Will the (increased) size of your company give you a competitive

> Once a company develops a brand name and gains a large enough percentage of the market share they are in a better position to control pricing and quality standards across the industry.

advantage, or is growth simply a desirable result you expect to achieve from a successful business strategy? If growth is simply the by-product of a successful strategy then it is not, at that point, effective as a differentiator for your business.

6. *Short-Term Profit*: Profit-driven businesses are consistently in a "harvesting" mode. These businesses choose to delay or reduce significant investments in themselves by setting high priorities on short-term profit margins. These businesses generally see the investor as the primary customer and the return on investment the indicator of success. Profit-driven companies are generally being prepared for sale, are focused on increasing the value of the stock, or the owner is winding down the business.

All businesses need to make decisions that are financially responsible, and profit is an appropriate motivation for being in business. But Profit as a top differentiator means that short-term profits become one of your major decision-making criteria. Short-Term Profit as a strategy is generally not sustainable in the long-term. Wanting your company to be profitable does not make Short-Term Profit your differentiator. Ask yourself: Is Short-Term Profit, at the expense of other considerations, your goal? Or is profit the result you would like to see by strategically positioning your business and as a result enhancing your company's overall success? If profit is simply the expected result of your company's success then, at this point, it is not necessarily one of your top differentiators.

It is difficult to provide a hotel that utilizes Short-Term Profit as one of their top differentiators because it tends to be a short-term strategy, and not one that can be maintained for long. However, many of us have known when we were staying in such a hotel. There tends to be significant delayed maintenance and lower than satisfactory staff service.

> Profit driven companies are generally being prepared for sale, are focused on increasing the value of the stock, or the owner is winding down the business.

7. *Method of Sale*: We all have to have some way of selling our services, but to make Method of Sale one of your top differentiators you must find a way to sell your services that other companies in your industry are not effectively using. Companies that have found an innovative way of making a sale can turn that method into a competitive advantage. Some alternative methods of sales include: time-shares, online catalogs, multi-level marketing organizations, and more recently, automated shopping services.

....

Companies that have found an innovative way of making a sale can turn that method into a competitive advantage.

An example of a hotel that uses Method of Sale as one of their top differentiators would be the Marriot through their strategic alliance with American Airlines. Together they offer vacation packages and frequent flyer miles for hotel stays. Successful companies from other industries that use Method of Sale as one of their top differentiators include: West Marine, Amazon.com, and Amway.

8. *Distribution Method*: A Distribution Method is a way of providing multiple services or products through a distribution channel to the same or similar markets. The way an organization distributes products and services may be one of its top differentiators and as a result create a competitive advantage. For example, distributing products through wholesale channels, duty free stores, and buying clubs. Once a distribution network has been developed, the organization can capitalize on it by using the distribution network to deliver additional products and services.

An example of a hotel that uses Distribution Method as one of their top differentiators is the Oaks at Ojai. This hotel provides a full range of spa products and services as well as a meal plan, education, and recreation. They are now expanding to offer seminars, cruises, books and tapes, as well as conference facilities. Successful companies from other industries that use Distribution Method as one of their top differentiators include: First Care Medical, Victoria's Secret, and Amway.

9. *Technological Advantage*: Technology-driven companies ensure they are breaking through in advance of the competition with leading edge technologies. This is not the same as using applied technology, i.e., having a Web page or e-mail access. Technology-driven companies use technology as a strategic advantage. A company that differentiates itself through Technology maintains its competitive advantage by continuing to invest in, develop, or use technology not already in common use throughout their industries.

> A Strategic Choice results from applying the differentiators to your business.

Ten years ago, all a hotel had to do to use Technology as a top differentiator was to offer access to a fax machine. Five years ago it had to provide data-ports. Now it needs to provide computer workstations and video-conferencing facilities. To compete on the basis of technology tomorrow they may need to offer "virtual company services" or "data-mining capacity." Successful companies from other industries that use Technology as one of their top differentiators include: 3M, Honda, and Canon.

A Strategic Choice results from applying the differentiators to your business. Because there are nine differentiators, we recommend you generate a minimum of nine Strategic Choices (one Strategic Choice for each differentiator). Most of our clients come up with twice that number. Every reordering and reprioritization of your Strategic Choices results in a new strategy, a new Vision for you and your business. There are millions of ways to combine nine Strategic Choices! How many choices have you and your management team been able to envision or see?

For the business leader success is a choice. That means you, as your business' leader, must consider where to be successful: in which market, with which products or services, using which business strategies. Your business is continuously faced with multiple choices, competing opportunities, and countless ways to invest your limited time, money, and energy.

Some of these choices and opportunities may take you where you want to go, others will not. How do you know which opportunities to choose? How do you differentiate yourself from your competition? Why should customers choose to do business with you? Strategic decision-making is a process for generating, selecting, prioritizing, and developing your choices into a workable and compelling Vision. Your Vision then becomes the focal point toward which you steer your business.

The most important tip we can give business leaders, as a result of our 15 years of strategic planning experience, is to fully understand and appreciate your choices before you choose. Many business leaders only identify three of four possible directions for their business before they make a decision. These three of four choices are generally based on what they have already done/tried, what the competition is doing, or the latest management trend touted by the popular press. The result of selecting from a limited group of off-the-rack choices is a limited Vision.

Taking the time to fully develop your ideas into Strategic Choices provides a solid foundation from which to develop a compelling business Vision. Your Vision is shaped by your selected and prioritized Strategic Choices. Each different prioritization of Strategic Choices will take your business in a slightly different direction. The number one responsibility of every business owner is the selection and prioritization of Strategic Choices, resulting in a business Vision. But remember, the first step is to really know what your Strategic Choices are; then you are better prepared to make decisions that make good business sense.

Strategic decision-making is a process for generating, selecting, prioritizing, and developing your choices into a workable and compelling Vision.

Differentiator Guidelines

The differentiators describe the basic ways business compete. They are used to see new options for your business and to appreciate and analyze what is driving your opportunities and investments. To better understand how the differentiators work, here are some guidelines.

◆ All successful companies invest in each of the differentiators (to at least the minimal standards in any particular
industry). Investing in a particular differentiator above
industry norms results in true market differentiation.

◆ The differentiators already drive your company's decision-making, whether or not you deliberately chose and
prioritized them.

◆ Each differentiator represents one or more potential
strategies for positioning a profitable company.

◆ Each differentiator is effective some of the time. No differentiator is effective all of the time.

◆ A competitive advantage can be achieved by selecting a
differentiator (or series of differentiators) your competition is currently not using.

◆ Each differentiator (or combination of differentiators)
represents another possible way for you to design and
position your company.

◆ Differentiators are directly linked to resource allocation
and day-to-day decision-making.

◆ The only strategy that consistently does not work is
choosing not to decide on your strategic priorities.

For clarity here is an in-depth look at the Differentiator Guidelines.

All Successful Companies Invest in Each of the Differentiators

No matter what industry you are in, you have an investment of
resources (time, energy, and money) in each of the differentiators.

◆ You have a market that you respond and sell products to,
so you are to some degree Market Responsive.

◆ You have some level of expertise, so you are to some
degree Product or Service Superiority-driven.

◆ You have developed systems to efficiently produce and
reproduce your products and services, so you are to
some degree Production Efficient.

....

A competitive advantage
can be achieved by
selecting a differentiator
(or series of differentiators) your competition is
currently not using.

- ◆ Because your business has grown you have experienced to some degree the benefits of increasing your market-share by being Market Dominance driven.

- ◆ Undoubtedly you make some decisions based solely on receiving or reserving short-term profits, so you are to some degree Profit driven.

- ◆ Your business has some natural or human resources, in the forms of personnel (and their reputations) or controlled access to a natural resource such as your business location.

- ◆ You have a way to sell your services or products, so you are to some degree driven by your Method of Sale.

- ◆ You have a way to distribute your services or products, so you are to some degree driven by your Method of Distribution.

- ◆ No business gets by today without some use of technology. Every business is to some degree driven by Technology.

How you prioritize the differentiators, which ones receive the lion's share of resources, defines your business strategy and the direction your business will evolve. Investing in a particular differentiator above industry norms results in true differentiation.

The Differentiators Are Already Driving Your Company's Decision-Making

Businesses that do not deliberately select and prioritize their differentiators often expend their resources haphazardly and inconsistently. As a consequence they have little forward momentum. Choosing to harness the power of the differentiators means focusing your energies and moving consistently forward in a direction that you have predetermined is right for you and your business.

The differentiators act like engines that power your business, and like engines they need fuel. One way to appreciate the role

....

The differentiator already drive your business.

of the differentiators in your business is to look at what you have been fueling; in other words, where have you invested in your business? To find out what is driving your business today, "follow the money."

The resources required to strengthen, expand, or maintain dominance for each of the differentiators are always competing for a piece of your business' budget. The differentiators have played a significant role in your past (and current) decision-making. To better understand the impact of the differentiators on your company, recall decisions you have made in the past that favored each one of them. You will begin to see more clearly how the differentiators represent opportunities for investing, making money, and creating a strategic advantage. Use Worksheet 5 to review your investments over the past 24 months and get a sense of what is really driving your business.

....

The differentiators act like engines that power your business, and like engines they need fuel.

Each Differentiator Represents One or More Potential Strategies for Positioning a Profitable Company

Even though Short-Term Profit is one of the differentiators, it is only one of many ways to strategically position a profitable company. You can be highly profitable by positioning yourself as having a superior product in your industry, or by meeting the needs of a specific market, and developing products or services to meet their needs. In fact, each of the differentiators could be used to lead or support a profitable strategy. The long-term profitability of a company is often more dependent on the development of a well-founded business strategy than it is on allowing profit to drive your decision-making.

All of the differentiators and their resulting business strategies require an investment of capital to sustain themselves as competitive advantages. For example, after over five years of being in business Amazon.com has still not recorded a profit although its stock value continues to rise and investors are still sticking with the company. Presumably this is because those investors appreciate the value of Amazon.com's strategy

WORKSHEET 5: Review Your Investments of Time, Energy, and Money in Your Business

Expenditure or investment _____

What did you want to achieve by this investment? _____

_____

Which of your business capabilities was enhanced by this investment? _____

_____

Expenditure or investment _____

What did you want to achieve by this investment? _____

_____

Which of your business capabilities was enhanced by this investment? _____

_____

Expenditure or investment _____

What did you want to achieve by this investment? _____

_____

Which of your business capabilities was enhanced by this investment? _____

_____

(which based on the name as well as their actions includes Market Domination and Method of Sale). The investors have confidence that Amazon.com will be able to stop investing so heavily in establishing market dominance, product development, and infrastructure and will ultimately become a very profitable company.

Each Differentiator is Effective Some of the Time

Chapter 4 described how Amazon.com carved out a unique market niche by using the Internet as a method for selling books. Their highly effective strategy needed to be revisited when Barnes & Noble, in essence, copied their Method of Sale. This is in fact a frequent occurrence. When you are successful, others will notice and the competition will copy you. This is why we say each differentiator is effective some of the time. No differentiator is effective all of the time. Be careful of industry experts who sell the same strategy to you, your competitors, and everyone else. This "me too" approach to strategy actually turns a specific differentiator away from being a competitive advantage to becoming just another way to keep up. A differentiator can give you a competitive advantage so long as your competition does not copy it or you operationalize it better than they do. Just like death and taxes, you can be sure that if you come up with a great strategy, someone will eventually copy it.

One example is beer. Do you remember when finding a local microbrew was a unique experience? Over the past five years almost every town in the U.S. (and in many other countries) grew its own local microbrew. Even many of the national and international beer producers now offer a microbrew product. Once your number one differentiator has been copied you have to revisit your strategy to develop a new competitive advantage. This can be done by replacing your top differentiator, finding a new way to use that differentiator, and/or reprioritizing your second, third, and fourth differentiators. The fact that each differentiator is only effective some of the time is one reason that the differentiators of every business tend to evolve and change over time.

Any differentiator can be effective within a specific industry, in a specific geographic area, for a specific time. However, when a differentiator becomes too popular it loses much of its effectiveness. Remember the purpose of a business strategy is to differentiate your business from others in your industry. If everyone is using the same strategy then it is very difficult to stand out from

> When you are successful, others will notice and the competition will copy you.

the crowd. For example, quality experienced a huge groundswell of popularity in the early 1980s. But if everyone claims to be selling the highest quality, then quality loses a lot of its selling power and customers will look for secondary characteristics that truly differentiate between you and your competition. For example, if two companies produce products that are perceived as being of equal quality then the customer becomes interested in which of the products is less expensive, can be delivered faster, or some other distinguishing factor.

Remember the purpose of a business strategy is to differentiate your business from others in your industry.

A business strategy and the differentiators from which it stems is effective some of the time, not all of the time. Fortunately you can combine and prioritize your Strategic Choices in so many different ways that the possible combination of strategies, for any business, numbers in the millions.

Each Combination of Differentiators Represents Another Potential Way to Successfully Design and Position Your Company

Differentiators are used to identify and generate Strategic Choices. A business strategy is composed of more than a single Strategic Choice. Using a combination of selected and prioritized Strategic Choices, powered by their associated differentiators, forms a strategy. Because the nine differentiators are in effect in every business, the important issue is "which" differentiator do you give the highest priority to. Say that in 1985, the differentiators behind Bob Inkman's four highest priority Strategic Choices were Market Responsive, Method of Sale, Production Efficiency, and Market Dominance. He distributed his resources accordingly and proportionately to develop, strengthen, and maintain the capabilities and characteristics representing each of these differentiators. At that point customers came to Bob because his was a "do it all" (Market Responsive) kind of shop that produced medium quality printing quickly and at a fair price (Production Efficiency). He depended on his high profile location to attract customers (Natural Resources) and he reinvested his profits to grow the business and capture more market share (Market Dominance).

A Competitive Advantage Can Be Achieved by Selecting a Differentiator (or Series of Differentiators) the Competition Is Currently Not Using

How do the majority of companies respond to their competitors? They look at what their competitors are offering or doing and then try to compete on pretty much the same basis. Everyone in our industry uses CAD drawing now; we better use CAD drawings. Everyone in our industry provides drive-through windows; we better offer a drive-through window. Everyone in our industry has a Web page; we better invest in a Web page. This "me too" management style tends to ensure your company is always just a little behind the pack, and restricts it to remaining there.

Take a different tack when analyzing your competition. Assess what Strategic Choices your competition is investing in and then plan to do something different. Find a Strategic Choice that is not effectively leveraged in your industry.

> ....
> Assess what Strategic
> Choices your
> competition is
> investing in and then
> plan to do something
> different.

Differentiators Are Directly Linked to Resource Allocation and Operational Decision-Making

Whatever the greatest share of your resources is invested in, generally tends to drive your business. You say your strategy is to create customer retention by selling more products to your current customers; however, your sales incentive systems favor new customers. You say you are committed to the quality of your services; however, your budget is larger for technology than staff training and customer service efforts. You advertise that you are superior providers in a specific service area, however, most of your Research & Development resources go to developing ancillary products outside your stated area of expertise. Your advertising suggests you bring agile solutions to your customers, yet most of your services are process-laden.

Your strategy drives your operational decision-making, resource allocation, and any incentive systems you may have. If you want to grow, increase the incentive to achieve gross volumes of sales.

If you want to strengthen your distribution channels, allocate resources to do so. If you want to be known as the superior product in your industry, invest in employee training and quality control systems. Your strategy provides the context for all day-to-day decision-making and expenditures of resources.

The Only Strategic Decision that Consistently Does Not Work is Not Deciding *on Your Strategic Priorities*

························

A business without a strategy is like a ship with no one at the helm.

This is the most fatal strategic flaw a business leader can make. A sign outside an automobile mechanics shop reads, "We specialize in foreign and American cars." There are no other types of cars! Clearly they are not specialists. This is an example of a business that has no strategy, no clearly laid-out priorities.

A business without a strategy is like a ship with no one at the helm. If the wind happens to blow from the north then the boat goes south. If the boat is headed toward the rocks there is no one to change its course. When a storm comes up the vessel is unprepared. If the boat reaches its destination it does so mostly by luck and by the most circuitous route.

The differentiators are at work in your business already. If you do not deliberately choose a strategy, then the choice will be made for you inconsistently and unconsciously. Make your decision-making process deliberate and intentional.

Developing Strategic Choices

The differentiators are tools to appreciate how businesses compete. To get value from them requires applying the differentiators to your business and the opportunities available to you, to come up with viable Strategic Choices. Figure 5.1 illustrates the relationship between differentiators and Strategic Choices.

As you go through the process of developing Strategic Choices keep in mind the following points:

FIGURE 5.1: The Relationship between Differentiators and Strategic Choices

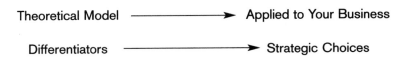

- ◆ Generate at least one viable Strategic Choice for each differentiator.
- ◆ Concentrate on the building blocks of strategy — Strategic Choices.
- ◆ There are two ways to generate a Strategic Choice.

Generate at Least One Viable Strategic Choice for Each Differentiator

It is important to consider and anticipate how you could apply each of the differentiators to your business to create a strategic advantage. It seems obvious when you first start applying the differentiators, how your business could compete by being Market Responsive, Product Efficient, or Product Superiority-driven. However, the process becomes more challenging and more rewarding the further down the list of differentiators you go.

Many businesses do not look past the first three or four differentiators (Market Responsive, Product or Service Superiority, Production Efficiency, or Human/Natural Resources). If you put a team of business leaders in a room and ask them what characteristics they use today to set themselves apart from the competition, most will offer examples relating to the first four differentiators.

Applying the last four or five differentiators to your business (Market Dominance, Short-Term Profit, Method of Sales, Distribution Method, Technological advantage) is likely to create a strategic advantage that has seen little if any use in your industry. It is for this reason that we suggest you come up with at least one viable Strategic Choice for each differentiators.

If you find it difficult to find a new way to differentiate your business, take the time to look again, because it is here where the treasure is buried. Leave the beaten track behind. Employ the rules generally associated with "brainstorming" (see Chapter 10) for this part of the process. Do not limit the possibilities; withhold your immediate judgments, and open yourself to strategic insights. Later in the process you will have ample opportunity to cull through your list before combining and prioritizing your Strategic Choices into your ultimate Vision.

Concentrate on the Building Blocks of Strategy — Strategic Choices

It is important at this step in the process to concentrate simply on creating the building blocks that later will be used in putting together your strategy. Often, clients try to create a whole strategy driven by a single differentiator. This is akin to building a house with one single very large brick.

Consider this snapshot of a car dealership located near a major university and see if you can figure out their Strategic Choices. Throughout the years the dealership has evolved to offer short-term lease programs of mid-sized and economy cars to meet students (and their parents) needs. It also sells cars that have been previously leased at affordable prices.

Looking at the snapshot of this dealership, the following four Strategic Choices with their associated differentiators can be extrapolated.

1. Focus on the needs of university students and faculty (Market Responsive).

2. Offer short-term lease programs (Method of Sale).

3. Resell previously leased cars (Distribution Method).

4. Focus on affordable product (Production Efficiency).

If you find it difficult to find a new way to use a differentiator for your business or industry, take the time to look again, because it is here where the treasure is buried.

Once you have taken a complete picture and separated it into Strategic Choices, with their associated differentiators, you can start to play with what the business might look like if you add a new Strategic Choice or simply re-prioritize the existing ones. Consider what would change about the business if you added just one different element, such as a financing program. Or, if you switched the order of the current Strategic Choices for example, you could make the reselling of leased vehicles your number one priority and offer that service to other leasing companies.

> Consider what would change about the business if you added just one different element, such as a financing program.

Gain strategic insights into your business by identifying each of the individual elements within your current business strategy. You are then prepared to reorder or change those elements to create a new business Vision.

If you try to adjust a strategy before you understand how it is put together you will probably not have as much success. Keep looking at the trees; forget the forest. Continue, for now, working with the building blocks of business strategy, your Strategic Choices.

There Are Basically Two Ways to Generate a Strategic Choice

There are basically two ways to generate a Strategic Choice and we recommend you use them both. Both methods serve the same purpose; they simply approach the subject from opposite directions. Using both methods will ensure your list of Strategic Choices is comprehensive. The first method is to take an existing capability or an opportunity that has presented itself, and understand how to power it by applying a differentiator. Bob Inkman and the printing press example, earlier in this chapter, demonstrate this method.

The second approach is to start with a differentiator and then find a unique way of applying it to your business or industry. Bob's search for a new Method of Sale exemplifies this method. He succeeded by identifying a way to make it easy for customers to modify, submit, and pay for printing projects online.

Use the differentiators to identify at least nine Strategic Choices that could realistically position your business. For example, a fictional, fast food franchise called Good & Delicious used the differentiators to identify the following Strategic Choices they could use to position their growing business for success:

1. **Market Responsive:**
   A. Respond to the needs of young families.
   B. Respond to the needs of landlords/developers.
   C. Respond to the needs of young adults.

2. **Product or Service Superiority:**
   A. Strengthen superiority and reputation in quality customer service.
   B. Build superiority in designing successful store fronts.
   C. Leverage our superiority and reputation in field operations management.

3. **Production Efficiency:**
   A. Reduce internal costs and increase consistency through stabilizing the workforce.
   B. Reduce internal costs and increase consistency by offering a limited product menu.
   C. Reduce internal costs and increase consistency by building dual branding in our locations.

4. **Human or Natural Resources:**
   A. Strengthen and retain beachside locations.
   B. Strengthen and retain our human resources through profit sharing and incentives.

5. **Market Dominance:**
   A. Dominate the market through mergers and acquisitions.
   B. Dominate the market by offering competitive pricing.
   C. Dominate the market by developing multiple outlets in a limited market area.

> Use the differentiators to identify at least nine Strategic Choices that could be used to realistically position your business.

6. **Short-Term Profit:**

   A. Increase profits by focusing on soft drink products.

   B. Increase profits by analyzing the profitability of different locations.

7. **Method of Sale:**

   A. Increase the number of sales through offering customer samples.

   B. Increase the number of sales by offering a franchising model.

8. **Method of Distribution:**

   A. Increase the number of sales to a customer by expanding our merchandising program.

   B. Increase the number of sales to a customer by offering combo meal.

9. **Technology:**

   A. Develop technological solutions to support the backroom decision-making.

This fast food franchise has identified 21 solid Strategic Choices by redefining the differentiators and applying them to their specific opportunities. It is only after you have identified a minimum of nine solid Strategic Choices, that you are prepared to begin combining them to create a viable and compelling Vision.

> It is only after you have identified a minimum of nine solid Strategic Choices, that you are prepared to begin combining them to create a viable and compelling Vision.

Costs and Benefits of Each Differentiator

Appreciating the costs and benefits, or advantages and disadvantages, of each of your Strategic Choices prepares you to make good solid strategic decisions. Use the following list of costs and benefits that are generally associated with each differentiator to better understand the costs and benefits of your Strategic Choices.

Market Responsive

Typical costs:

- New products and services
- Loss of control over your schedule
- Investment in market research and customer surveys
- Competing demands on staff
- Difficulties in developing routines or policies
- High marketing expenses

Typical benefits:

- Happy customers and return customers
- Creative, responsive work environment
- Constant innovations
- Ability to find new solutions to meet customer's needs

Products or Service Superiority

Typical costs:

- Constant improvement of product to stay ahead in industry
- Higher cost of providing the highest-cost products or service
- Most of your investment is in one area of expertise

Typical benefits:

- Excellent reputation as the best
- Ability to charge more money for your products and services
- Strong customer referrals
- Greater consistency from the customer's perspective
- Simplified marketing requirements

Production Efficiency

Typical costs:

- Repetitive and limited product line
- Possible reduction in quality and innovation
- Loss of innovation or motivation

Typical benefits:

- Better competitive pricing and lower-cost products

- Consistency of work environment
- Ability to use automation technology

Natural and Human Resources

Typical costs:
- Dependence on people for reputation
- Challenge controlling quality and consistency
- Changing interests and motivations of key people
- Higher expenses for human resources

Typical benefits:
- Creative energy
- Doing what you love
- Relationships with customers

Market Dominance

Typical costs:
- Decline in quality and consistency
- Problems with cash flow
- Need for systems to be documented and policies to be made
- Loss of commitment or relationships among co-workers and employees

Typical benefits:
- Resources to purchase in quantity
- Clear accounting systems to measure success
- Ability to control larger portions of the market share
- Opportunities for expansion and promotion of human resources

Short-Term Profit

Typical costs:
- Focus on the short-term when decision-making
- Delayed maintenance and related ongoing costs
- Delays in investing in the company
- Lack of emphasis in the area of product innovation
- Possible negative impact on expansion into new markets

Typical benefits:
- Easy-to-use systems for measuring success
- Motivational to people who receive a share of the profits

- Strong position when anticipating a harsh business environment
- More choices about how to change in the future

Method of Sales

Typical costs:

- Fickleness of buyers
- Impact of world changes on your specific method of sale
- Lack of association with a specific product or service

Typical benefits:

- Addition of new products within your sales system
- A strong and qualified network of sales people
- New ways to reach a stagnant buying market

Distribution Method

Typical costs:

- Distribution system may limit markets
- Investment of up-front resources to develop
- Customers removed from the provider

Typical benefits:

- Ease of adding new products or services easily
- Ease of getting products to customers quickly
- Easy resale to a buyer who requires a distribution network

Technological Advantage

Typical costs:

- Hard and expensive to stay in the lead
- Overpriced prototypes with technological bugs
- Quick application of new technologies
- Investment in research and development
- Buyer education

Typical benefits:

- Company fame
- Ability to sell your idea
- Name your own price

Appreciating the relative advantages and disadvantages of each Strategic Choice is a good way to keep your feet on the ground while your eyes are searching the horizon for a new Vision.

For example, a company explored the specific costs and benefits to be expected from implementing the following Strategic Choice:

Distribution Method: To develop strategic alliances with vendors to access products.

Costs:
- Limited product mix for each vendor source
- Continuous evaluation and negotiations with vendors
- Research and Development improvement costs
- Keeping up with regulatory requirements
- High demand of time to maintain relationships

Benefits:
- Ability to have a distinct product line
- Enjoy long term working relationships/alliances
- Create loyalty with customers
- Creates options for direct sales
- Our partners could also feed us business

Know Your Choices Before You Decide

As stated earlier, knowing what your choices are, before you decide, is an essential component of good decision-making. Why is it important to know your Strategic Choices before you decide?

- Increase your options and create a new vision for yourself and business.

- When you have more options, you have more strategic insights and make better decisions.

- There is great benefit from collecting ideas from multiple sources (employees, customers, business advisers, and other industries).

Once you have generated your Strategic Choices, the next question is how to choose from among them, and how to combine them to form a business strategy. Figure 5.2 demonstrates the progression from the theoretical model to the practical application to the selection of your business strategy.

Chapter 6 focuses on the criteria you apply to make these decisions with clarity and confidence, and to ensure that you select a viable business strategy.

FIGURE 5.2: Forming a Strategy

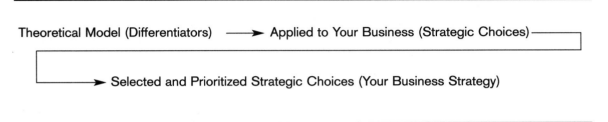

Theoretical Model (Differentiators) ⟶ Applied to Your Business (Strategic Choices)

Selected and Prioritized Strategic Choices (Your Business Strategy)

The Four Perspectives

· ·

· · · · · · · · · · · · · · · · · · · ·

Developing a
comprehensive list of
Strategic Choices
provides you with the
input essential for
gaining insights into new
possibilities and is vital
for making solid
strategic decisions.

In the last chapter we talked about Strategic Choices and the nine ways in which businesses compete. We also demonstrated how matching a characteristic or capability with each of the differentiators creates Strategic Choices. The purpose was to develop at least one Strategic Choice for each differentiator. Developing a comprehensive list of Strategic Choices provides you with the input essential for gaining insights into new possibilities and is vital for making solid strategic decisions.

Once you have a fully developed list of Strategic Choices the question then becomes: How do you decide? By what criteria do you make such an important decision? How do you choose the right course for your business? Decisions of such consequence require using more than one criterion. In fact, before you decide, we suggest you consider your business and the strategic opportunities revealed in the previous chapter, from four key perspectives.

- ◈ Core Capabilities
- ◈ Market Forecast

◆ Competitive Analysis

◆ Personal Definition of Success

This chapter leads you through an analysis of your Strategic Choices based on these four key perspectives. A perspective is simply a different way of looking at a problem or challenge. Considering your business from several different perspectives mirrors the decision-making process of a visionary business leader. The four perspectives presented in this book establish the criteria that must be met in order to create a viable and compelling business strategy.

To satisfy the requirements of each perspective, four Strategic Choices are selected from your master list of Strategic Choices. The result is four sets of four Strategic Choices. Each set fulfills the criteria established by one of the perspectives. For each of these sets of Strategic Choices a scenario or picture is drawn of what the business would look like if you were to use those selected Strategic Choices to form a business strategy. Viewing and understanding your business from the four perspectives reveals a business strategy that is fueled by the owner's dreams and values, is anchored in the businesses strengths, limits the competition, and is based on anticipated market needs.

> Considering your business from several different perspectives mirrors the decision-making process of a visionary business leader.

Core Capabilities

Core Capabilities are the characteristics, capabilities, and qualities that your business successfully leverages today. Consider these questions.

◆ Do you provide a variety of services to a particular market? If so, what market?

◆ Are you the expert in your industry? If so, what is your area of superiority?

◆ Do your customers choose you because you offer the lowest prices? If so, how do you keep your costs down?

◆ Do your customers choose you because you offer the quickest service? If so, what systems do you have in place that enable you to do so?

- ◈ Has your company grown to where its name is synonymous with the products your industry offers?

- ◈ Do you have a method of selling or distributing your services that puts you ahead of the competition, if so, what is it?

- ◈ What is it about your business that causes customers to choose your products, right now?

The answers to these questions point to the strategies, the capabilities you presently leverage today. The strategies that currently account for your company's success are your Core Capabilities. Core Capabilities do not include those things you want to be or think you should be. They are just a clear, impartial, objective assessment of who you are today, and the capabilities you are effectively able to demonstrate.

Why is building on your Core Capabilities important to your long-term success?

- ◈ You have already invested in the people, systems, and tools required to support your Core Capabilities.

- ◈ Your Core Capabilities are the foundation of your current success with your customers.

You Have Already Invested In the People, Systems, and Tools Required to Support Your Core Capabilities

After concluding the strategic decision-making process, the vast majority of businesses adjust their course rather than radically alter it. They take advantage of many of the systems and tools they already have in place. Take advantage of the systems and tools already working well for you, by building on the capabilities that have contributed to your current success.

For example, one of Starbucks' top differentiators was Market Dominance as exemplified by their slogan "2000 by 2000." There are many ways they could have accomplished this goal, and wisely they built on their Core Capabilities, specialty coffee

> Take advantage of the systems and tools already working well for you, by building on the capabilities that have contributed to your current success.

drinks. Another of the Core Capabilities they built on was a well-established Method of Sales in the form of their successful coffee-bar storefronts.

Your Core Capabilities Are the Foundation of Your Current Success with Your Customers

> Building on your Core Capabilities ensures a smooth transition as you adjust your course and ultimately your sales towards fulfillment of your Vision.

Many of Applied Business Solutions, Inc.'s clients are successful businesses that have reached a plateau and are looking for a way to take the "next step." Just like them, you would be duly hesitant to throw away the hard work that has lead to your current success. You will find that you can utilize the capabilities you are good at today as the foundation for where you want to take your business tomorrow. If you have gotten this far, then it is safe to assume that you have created some kind of market identity that your customers recognize, and you provide your customers with services or products they are familiar with. Building on your Core Capabilities ensures a smooth transition as you adjust your course and ultimately your sales towards fulfillment of your Vision.

It can be helpful to understand the evolution of your business' Core Capabilities. As your business has developed and grown, your Core Capabilities have and will, continue to change. The example below charts how Bob Inkman's differentiators have evolved over time.

Bob Inkman's Differentiators (Core Capabilities) as They Evolved Over Time

	1985	1990	1995	2000
1.	Market Responsive	Market Responsive	Method of Sale	Product Superiority
2.	Method of Sale	Production Efficient	Product Superiority	Human Resources
3.	Production Efficient	Market Dominance	Distribution Method	Short-Term Profit
4.	Market Dominance	Method of Sale	Market Dominance	Technology

1985. Bob started off, as many businesses do, by being somewhat Market Responsive. To him this meant responding to the needs of the entire market. This makes sense because new small businesses are often cash poor and willing to take whatever work walks in the door, regardless of what they do best or are best prepared to do. Though it was expensive, he located the business in a strip mall that gave him a lot of visibility and walk-in business. He bought the right equipment, and trained his employees to provide quick service for moderate price and quality. He reinvested a fair proportion of profits into a marketing campaign with the ultimate Vision of growing to capture 25 percent of the printing market in his region.

1990. Bob still says "yes" to virtually every project that comes in the door. He notices that what his customers seem to want most is competitive pricing and that they are willing to sacrifice (to some degree) quality to get it. So instead of remodeling the store as a friend suggested, he invests in increasing his production efficiency through the purchase of a preowned press that can be used for longer runs and is easy for a relatively unskilled employee to manage. He continues to reinvest profits to keep the business growing. He hires a sales representative to beef up sales.

1995. His sales representative was so successful that he added two more and they are actively involved in local trade and business associations. Since so much of his business over the past ten years has been business cards and brochures, Bob's shop has developed a reputation for providing superior start-up collateral. When his sales team goes out prospecting, the top service they present is their fairly inexpensive, two-color brochures. Bob begins experimenting with offering other business supplies for the small home office. He continues to invest in growth and wants to open another printing operation in an industrial park.

2000. Bob's shop is now known in the local professional associations as the place to go for start-up collateral. His team has developed a consulting reputation. They are known for their commitment to finding start-up solutions to effectively launch entrepreneurs with style. Bob feels that with his new tighter focus and referral reputation he no longer needs to invest in aggressive marketing. He instead is investing in desktop design capacity and computer-to-print technology.

It has been said that change is the only constant in the universe. Undoubtedly, your business priorities and personal goals have changed. Take a few minutes to think about how your business has evolved by completing Worksheet 6.

Bob Inkman's current Strategic Choices are also his Core Capabilities. The same is true for your business. The actual Strategic Choices that currently drive your business are your Core Capabilities.

We will use the fast food franchise Good & Delicious to demonstrate how to work with Strategic Choices. The following

---

WORKSHEET 6: Appreciate How Your Company's Strategic Choices Have Evolved

Record the evolution of your company's top Strategic Choices since it was started.

	19__	19__	19__	20__
1.				
2.				
3.				
4.				

Strategic Choices were chosen from Good & Delicious' master list as being an objective assessment of their current business strengths and capabilities:

2A. Strengthen and maintain superiority and reputation in quality customer service.

3B. Reduce internal costs and increase consistency through a limited product menu.

6A. Increase firm profits by focusing on soft drink products.

7A. Increase the number of sales by offering customer samples.

·····················

Each set of four selected and prioritized Strategic Choices will take your business in a different direction and as a result deliver your business to a different destination five to ten years from now.

Scenarios

The next step is to develop a scenario based on your Core Capabilities. Each set of four selected and prioritized Strategic Choices will take your business in a different direction and as a result deliver your business to a different destination five to ten years from now. We call that hypothetical destination a *scenario*. Several times during the strategic decision-making process we recommend you develop a scenario based on the Strategic Choices you are considering at the time.

The following is a scenario for Good & Delicious if it were to continue on its present course, and management were to continue investing primarily in their current Core Capabilities:

The company is a very simple straightforward design that can be easily replicated. It remains a smaller player in the fast food industry and may find that it eventually cannot produce the revenues required to lease prime real estate.

Acknowledging your Core Capabilities does not mean you have to maintain your present course. In fact the majority of our clients are not overly pleased with the insight they gained by identifying where they and their businesses are likely to wind up if they continue on their present courses. However, taking this perspective into account ensures that you are not unduly risking the blood, sweat, and tears you have invested in your business by turning your back on the successes that have brought it to where it is today. Chart a course for your business that is anchored in your Core Capabilities.

Market Forecast

....

Use industry trends, cycles, and other available data to gain a better understanding of how external factors strongly influence your company's success, both today and in the future.

A Market Forecast is the second perspective you should look from when developing a successful strategy. Market forecasting uses research to extrapolate the business climate in which you will be operating five to ten years from now. Use industry trends, cycles, and other available data to gain a better understanding of how external factors strongly influence your company's success, both today and in the future. You will use your understanding of these trends to position your business to meet forecasted market needs.

A data-driven forecast can help you prepare for the future, choose the best direction to take, and respond quickly when changes arise. It is important to be able to identify consistent patterns in your specific business climate and to be prepared to meet them. The goal is to anticipate potential problems, take advantage of useful business cycles, and select key indicators to track, which will tell you when the wind is shifting. In order to gain a competitive advantage, you as a business leader have a vital need to be not only aware of the present state of the market, but also to be prepared for predictable changes.

Market Forecasts can be used to:

- ✦ Identify how the marketplace is changing and anticipate how those changes will impact your business.

- ✦ Reveal new Strategic Choices for your industry.

- ✦ Educate the decision-makers on your team about the competition.

- ✦ Build a business barometer that alerts you to upcoming changes.

Identify How the Marketplace Is Changing and How Those Changes Will Impact Your Business.

The marketplace is always changing, and the assumptions you made when you began in your industry or with your business may be obsolete. How often do we really pick our heads up to do a comprehensive survey of the trends that impact us? Most of us are too immersed in day-to-day operational concerns to do a thorough job of tracking changes in the marketplace.

A good illustration of this is a travel agency that didn't see the airline commission caps coming and were caught in the wrong part of a staffing and growth cycle. The commission caps were not a closely held secret and were anticipated by many in the industry. This agency should have realized that their projected sales were about to be cut significantly. The smart agencies prepared for the commission caps by changing their service focus, introducing service fees, or identifying another Strategic Choice which provided them with a competitive advantage.

What happened to the typewriter manufacturers who didn't appreciate the coming impact of personal computers? How has the CPA industry been forced to change now that you can keep your accounting on sophisticated software that can also do your taxes? What is the impact on developers and the timber industry in the Pacific Northwest of putting salmon on the endangered species list? Most of these changes were easily forecasted but many businesses were caught by surprise. Some business owners bury their heads in the sand, fight change, or deny the potential severity of coming changes. Others see the change coming and proactively reposition their companies for ongoing success. Predicting the future with certainty is impossible but keeping your eyes open is a strategic skill and can position you way ahead of the competition. It is estimated that by the year 2010 Hispanics will overtake African Americans as the single largest minority in the U.S. What is your business doing to proactively position itself to meet the Spanish speaking market?

The environment in which ships sail (the ocean) and the environment in which you do business (the marketplace) share

> Predicting the future with certainty is impossible but keeping your eyes open is a strategic skill and can position you way ahead of the competition.

important characteristics. Most notable are the frequent and dramatic changes common to both. Many of these changes follow predictable cycles like the currents and the tides. Others of those changes come up quickly with little warning. However, for the aware observer the events leading up to those changes are often observable and predictable. In the business marketplace there are also patterns and cycles that can be relied on to repeat themselves. Reasonably accurate forecasts can be made from studying these patterns.

....

In the business marketplace there are also patterns and cycles that can be relied on to repeat themselves.

Most businesses are impacted by the following business cycles:

- ◆ *Economic cycles.* This includes the national and local economies, interest rates, inflation, and the buying power of your customers.

- ◆ *Population or demographic trends.* This cycle includes the age of the population, needs of the population, educational levels, and availability of trained workers.

- ◆ *Product maturation cycles.* Specifically, where is your particular product or service in the product maturation cycle? Products tend to start off relatively unsophisticated, with many distinguishing features, and with many different price points. They then tend to evolve into a commodity product that offers common features, and more consistent, consumer-sensitive pricing. Ultimately they again move toward differentiation.

  Consider the evolution of facial tissues as a classic example of a product maturation cycle. First someone trademarked a new product, "Kleenex™." Then others were able to quickly copy and market the facial tissue. Although the brand name of the inventor continues to be used to describe the product, there evolved little differentiation, besides packaging, between all brands of facial tissue. This is common to the commodity stage of product maturation. Recently there are budding examples of product differentiation including a product being marketed by Purely Cotton (an all cotton product) and advancements in lanolin laced facial tissues specifically for people with colds.

Personal computers also provide a good example of the product maturation cycle. When personal computers first came out there were a lot of different types, they were expensive, and there were problems with interconnectivity between computers and software. In the next cycle, the whole industry moved toward standardization. Most computers evolved to run most available software applications. Pricing became relatively uniform, taking into account features. The personal computer thus became a commodity product.

The introduction of the latest Macintosh (1999) may be the beginning of the third cycle of product maturation. Computer manufacturers are starting to strive for differentiation in an attempt to move their products beyond being a price-sensitive commodity. It doesn't matter if you are talking about the airline industry, computer manufacturers, professional services, or e-commerce, the evolution of the product maturation cycle in your industry is important to consider in the selection of your business strategy.

⬧ *Customer buying cycles.* Identify what is impacting your customers' buying decisions. How are social, environmental, and economic issues impacting them? Are they consolidating or spending? Are interest rates making it difficult for them to find investment capital to meet their growth plans? If your customers are consumers, how are they being impacted by transportation issues, taking care of their elderly parents, or sending their children off to college? Whatever is impacting your market will sooner than later have an impact on you.

⬧ *Industry cycles.* What are the changes within your industry? Are new high-tech materials available for building your products or providing services? Is there a new process available that your competition is using to standardize quality or reduce costs? Is there a lack of trained professionals available that results in an increase in your compensation requirements and eventually your service delivery costs?

....

Market forecasting is a very effective way to reveal new Strategic Choices for your industry.

Reveal New Strategic Choices for Your Industry

Market forecasting is a very effective way to reveal new Strategic Choices for your industry. A vocational training institute does a Market Forecast and notices that the largest growing sector of the population in the U.S. is Hispanic, many with English as a second language. Immediately they see how creating a new Strategic Choice around offering courses in Spanish could provide them with a competitive advantage. What Strategic Choices have you developed that position your firm to be successful in the future marketplace? Use your understanding of the trends impacting your industry and customers to identify new Strategic Choices for your business.

A construction management firm notices that clients are overwhelmed by the increased complexity of the preconstruction management process. They are the first to see a new Strategic Choice: to be specialists in preconstruction consultation. A waterworks manufacturer notices that existing water-works infrastructures in many major cities are deteriorating. They recognize this as an opportunity to develop a new Strategic Choice, by offering a full line of refurbishing products and processes. A CPA firm notices that 25 percent of their clients will need to transfer the ownership of their businesses in the next five years. In anticipation of this need they develop a new Strategic Choice that includes a comprehensive set of services to support business succession.

Educate the Decision-Makers in Your Company on Trends Impacting Your Industry

The process of preparing for the future, scanning the environment, and responding to it is a key business-leadership skill. Involving your management team in learning about market trends increases their willingness and ability to appreciate why your business priorities might need to change, and what the business may have to do to remain competitive in the future. In addition, it is often the supervisors and frontline employees who get the most direct contact and feedback concerning the changing face of your industry and the changing needs of your customers. These people may bring some very valuable insights to the table about where your industry is headed.

> The process of preparing for the future, scanning the environment, and responding to it is a key business-leadership skill.

A case in point is a business owner who has led a successful business for over 20 years. He was confident his company was heading in the right direction until one day he found it floundering and was totally caught off guard. There had been a major change in market needs, and he had not seen it. He was doubly disappointed when he learned that some key employees had seen it coming for months. Why hadn't they told him? They hadn't told him because they assumed he already knew. He had always kept his ideas about future market needs in his head, so in truth there had been no way for his team to know what the owner was or wasn't aware of.

When he did open up the conversation, it was too late. They instituted the required changes, but were forced to play catch-up, when only recently they had been the market leaders. Use a Market Forecast data-gathering process to build shared understanding, document conclusions, and gain consensus on the best way to position your business to meet forecasted market needs.

A Good Forecast also Functions as a Barometer

Everyone knows that it is impossible to predict the future. Some business leaders use this fact as an excuse to not make a forecast, but forecasting is valuable even when it is not totally accurate. You can use the trends on which you based your forecast to create a barometer that tracks and alerts you to forthcoming changes that directly affect your business.

A Market Forecast documents the trends that most impact your business and the directions in which those trends are moving. Developing a "business barometer" as an extension of your forecast is a relatively simple and highly rewarding project. Your business barometer records the indicators that alert you to changes in the trends that you have based your forecast on. It contains a list of resources that report on those indicators, and the frequency with which you should keep track of them.

In the above example if the business leader had written down and presented his understanding of upcoming market needs, his

---

Use a Market Forecast data-gathering process to build shared understanding, document conclusions, and gain consensus on the best way to position your business to meet forecasted market needs.

management team would have been able to point out the distinctions between what they were seeing and what the leader was thinking. If you keep your forecast in your head, it does not get exposed to the scrutiny of others, and as a result can take your business off-course, or cause you to miss an important opportunity. All market forecasting should be updated annually at a minimum to check its accuracy and to identify any new trends that the business should be anticipating and incorporating into their strategic decision-making process.

How to Create and Use a Market Forecast

Forecasting, sometimes called futuring, is both an art and a science. How you create your own Market Forecast depends on how much time and resources you are willing to invest. Some businesses use market research firms to do their Market Forecasts or sophisticated competitive intelligence software. Other businesses just "go with what they know" and take some time each year for the leadership of the business to sit down together and document the major trends impacting their industry and customers. The insights you receive from your forecasting depend on how much time and energy you put into it.

Regardless of the method you choose, documenting the changes you perceive coming to your market will put you miles ahead of the competition, many of whom do not document their assumptions about the future and as a result have no process for updating those assumptions.

Developing a Forecast on Your Own. You can do your own research to develop a forecast using information publicly available through libraries, bookstores, and the Internet. Our *Chart Your Own Course*® workbook contains detailed guidelines on how to create your own forecast using these kinds of resources.

Bookstores and libraries are full of resources to assist you in developing your market forecast. You can also find a wealth of descriptive data through the Internet.

The insights you receive from your forecasting depend on how much time and energy you put into it.

Even though data is available from many sources, it can be challenging to use. You may find conflicting reports, and with so many sources, the information you collect has varying degrees of accuracy. Don't get tangled up in the details of the data; your primary objective is to forecast the business environment you will be working in. Look for information that is specific to your industry. Let common sense be your guide.

Other ways of doing your own research include using publicly available, up-to-date resources. Local banks, newspapers, chambers of commerce, professional associations, and business schools often publish valuable information about the local market and financial projections. Your particular trade organizations and trade journals may publish articles on the future of your industry. These organizations tend to have fairly informative web sites or research departments. Many online services can give you up-to-the-minute forecasting information. Visit the *Chart Your Own Course*® Web site at www.appliedbizsolutions.com for links to valuable forecasting information.

If you do not have the time or inclination to do in-depth research, you'll still find it extremely valuable to use the knowledge you have already gained through your experiences in your industry. Use what you have learned by watching the news, reading the papers, and talking with business leaders, customers, and trusted advisers. Document your knowledge and intuition. The knowledge you have garnered through hard work and experience is the most valuable. Some of that knowledge is retained on an unconscious level and is referred to as intuition. Intuition is often a huge and untapped resource for the business leader.

You may choose to hire a market research firm. Although this is generally a more expensive option, it is often a good one. A market research firm can provide a comprehensive report on each specific area you have identified, and bring forward trends in areas you may not have been aware of that are impacting your business.

> Use what you have learned by watching the news, reading the papers, and talking with neighbors, customers, and trusted advisers.

What Do You Do With the Results of Your Market Forecast?

Use the results of your Market Forecast to strengthen your strategic decision-making. The Market Forecast is one of the four perspectives we suggest you use to choose the strategy for your business. Select and prioritize four Strategic Choices based on your market forecast. For example:

Good & Delicious selected the following Strategic Choices from their master list of Strategic Choices because these Strategic Choices best fulfill the needs identified in their Market Forecast:

....

Knowing what your competition is doing, or planning to do, enables you to choose a differentiating direction.

3A. Reduce internal costs and increase consistency through stabilizing the workforce.

2C. Strengthen superiority and reputation in field operations management.

8B. Increase the number of sales, to one customer by offering combo meals.

1B. Respond to the needs of landlords/developers.

The following is a potential scenario for Good & Delicious if it were to focus its time, energy, and resources in a strategy based solely on the Strategic Choices they selected in response to the Market Forecast:

This company would invest resources to have qualified, dedicated, and committed employees and as a result could supply trained employees to other fast food chains. They would build their superiority in the management of fast food restaurants. In addition, they saw the need to update their menus to offer nutritious meals to meet the needs of the aging population's priorities while ensuring substantial revenue per square foot and attractive concepts to meet the developer's needs.

Competitive Analysis

A Competitive Analysis is the third essential perspective from which you should consider your strategy. A Competitive

Analysis is the gathering of information regarding the characteristics and capabilities your competitors are, or are planning to invest in to create an advantage. Knowing what your competition is doing, or planning to do, enables you to choose a different direction. A direction that would really set your business apart from the rest. Completing a Competitive Analysis reveals the Strategic Choices that are under-utilized in your industry and thus presents an opportunity for you to create a unique competitive advantage.

Your Strategy Determines Who You Compete With

It is important to know what is going on in your industry.

A Competitive Analysis alerts you to which companies each of your Strategic Choices may put you in competition with. Understanding who is using each of your Strategic Choices enables you to choose a strategy that limits the competition. It is important to know what is going on in your industry. As time passes, competitors come and go, leaving gaps that you can fill and indicating pitfalls to be avoided.

The Competitive Analysis Tips You Off to New Strategic Choices

What are the Strategic Choices your competitors are using that you have not yet considered? Take note of the strategies that work effectively for the competition. Be sure those Strategic Choices are also on your list even if you do not intend to use them. Remember you can combine a Strategic Choice that works well for a competitor with several other Strategic Choices that are not available to your competitor, to create a unique business strategy.

What are the Strategic Choices your competition is *not* using? If your analysis reveals that no other competitor in your industry distinguishes themselves on the basis of Human Resources, you might want to explore how you could. Chances are your competitors aren't using a particular differentiator because companies in your industry have traditionally competed on some other basis. These under or un-utilized differentiators represent an opportunity for you to create a new competitive position within your industry.

Educate the Decision-Makers on Your Team about the Competition

Working together with the rest of the decision-makers in your company to analyze what the competition is doing will provide everyone on your team with a better understanding of the competitive marketplace, how you compare, and how you can best position your business as unique. The result is shared understanding and consensus on the best path to take. In fact others in your company may have more or different information about your competitors. They may have already worked for your competitors, or they may know people who work with the competition. Firsthand knowledge of your competitor's strategy is always better than information gleaned from public sources. You will be able to make your business stand out from your competition when you identify and prioritize a combination of Strategic Choices that are not currently being used effectively by others in your industry.

Completing a Competitive Analysis

The differentiators provide an excellent tool for understanding and categorizing the information you learn about your competitors. Identify what their differentiators are, and when possible, their corresponding Strategic Choices. The point is to look for strategies that are not in common use in your industry.

Review your competitors' products or services, marketing materials, and distribution networks to better understand their differentiators. There are many ways to gain access to your competitors' marketing and product information. You could ask your customers what they know about the competition. You could check out their Web page. Web pages are a significant resource to a company participating in a Competitive Analysis. You could call your competitors and ask them to send their marketing information. If you have the financial resources, you may choose to hire a market research firm to conduct your Competitive Analysis. By reviewing this information you should be able to determine what the top differentiators and Strategic Choices of your competition may be.

Review your competitors' products or services, marketing materials, and distribution networks to better understand how they have chosen to differentiate themselves.

Look for ways you can position yourself by creating a new combination of Strategic Choices, one that your competition is not currently offering. For instance, Anita Roddick, the founder of The Body Shop, came out of left field when she decided to make her products reasonably priced, environmentally sensitive, and accessible in neighborhood stores. Roddick wasn't kidding when she said, "I watch where the cosmetic industry is going and then I walk in the opposite direction." If you look at your competition and then choose to do what they do, you are following; you are not defining differentiating strategy. Finding a new way to offer your product or service often leads to defining a new strategy and competitive advantage. What new opportunities present themselves when you do not follow, but lead?

In his article, "Strategy as Revolution" published in the *Harvard Business Review*, Gary Hammel suggests that you are a rule maker, a rule taker, or a rule breaker. Major companies such as IBM, CBS, United Airlines, and Coca-Cola are market dominators and as a result are the rule makers. Next are the rule takers. These are the companies following behind these and other leaders. The examples Hammel gives include: Fujitsu, ABC, U.S. Air, and others. For the rule takers, or followers, life is hard. Imagine being Avis trying to catch up with Hertz. "We Try Harder" may be a great advertising slogan, but it is depressingly futile as a business strategy. We suggest you consider being a rule breaker. Identify a strategy not currently used effectively by your competition.

Good & Delicious chose the following four Strategic Choices because they are characteristics and capabilities that are not effectively being leveraged by other businesses in the fast food industry. As a result they represent a viable, differentiating strategy:

> 3A. Reduce internal costs and increase consistency through stabilizing the workforce.
>
> 4B. Strengthen and retain human resources through profit sharing and incentives.
>
> 7A. Increase the number of sales through offering customer samples.

Finding a new way to offer your product or service often leads to defining a new strategy and competitive advantage.

2C. Leverage our superiority and reputation in field operations management.

The following is a potential scenario for Good & Delicious if it were to invest solely in the above Strategic Choices:

This is a fast food industry leader who has taken a unique approach to managing and providing incentives to their human resources. This aggressive approach to human resource retention has allowed the company to provide consistent and cost effective service. In addition they approach consumers to introduce their products by giving away free samples. They export their winning strategy as consultants to other fast food companies.

Acknowledging the approach that most differentiates you from your competition does not mean you are required to take that course. It does mean that you may want to take those choices into consideration as you continue charting the right course for your business.

The importance you put on this or any of the four perspectives depends on where you really intend to take your business. If you are contemplating dominating your market, or franchising your concept or any other focus on market dominance that requires you grab market share from others, the importance of this perspective cannot be underestimated. However, if you are currently operating with about .1 percent of the market share in your region and you would be happy staying at this level, then this perspective may not have as significant of an impact on your final decisions. In either case, the importance of looking at your business strategy from this perspective is to give you insight into how you can position your business as unique, within your industry.

> Acknowledging the approach that most differentiates you from your competition does not mean you are required to take that course.

Owner's Personal Definition of Success (PDS)

How the business owner defines success personally directly impacts the business and must be taken into consideration when developing a comprehensive strategy. The owner's PDS is a combination of personal reasons for being in business, long-term business goals, personal values and motivations, and the energy level the owner is willing to invest in the business. When choosing the future destination for your business, it is important to weave your personal motivations and values into the decision-making process.

Incorporating your PDS into the planning process is key to turning your business into a vessel for achieving your dreams. Taking the time to consider the owner's personal lifestyle goals and objectives prior to deciding on a business strategy makes solid business sense.

What Is the Owner's Personal Definition of Success?

How success is defined depends on who is at the helm. For some, making fast money is success. For others, having something to leave to their children in the form of a business is more motivating. For still others, success means having a satisfying part-time job that affords them the lifestyle they enjoy.

Crayne Horton started the Fish Brewing Company because of his love of gourmet beverages. He integrates his personal concern and commitment to salmon habitat restoration by donating a percentage of sales from the company's Wild Salmon Pale Ale to the Save Our Wild Salmon organization. Mr. Horton has been heard to say "If there are no salmon, that means there is no clean water — and there's no good beer." Early in the year 2000 they will introduce another beer, Thornton Creek Ale, a portion of whose proceeds will be donated to the Thornton Creek Alliance.

The business grew dramatically until in 1997 it was ranked 81st in size among all U.S. commercial brewers and 10th among Washington state brewers in output (4,800 barrels).

In 1999, Horton hired a new CEO and stepped down from that position to become head of sales and marketing for the company. This was due partly to personal reasons, he had just become a parent and wanted to put less time into the business and partly to good solid business reasons. The business had grown beyond his ability to comfortably manage it, and stopped reaching projected revenue levels.

> How success is defined depends on who is at the helm.

In his new position, freed of administrative responsibilities, Horton makes better use of his enthusiasm, inventiveness, and entrepreneurial spirit. The company is now under the leadership of a professional business manager, operating within a disciplined plan. Sometimes achieving your PDS means giving up the helm.

Bigger is better and will make me happier! When you start to develop your PDS, watch out for the most common assumption business owners make: bigger is better. "If I enjoy sailing on a 25-foot boat, I will really love a 50-foot boat!" This misconception has led many a boat owner down an expensive path they later regretted. There is no direct relationship between the size of the boat and the amount of fun boaters have. In fact, many people prefer the responsiveness and lesser demands of a 25-foot boat to the responsibility and challenges of a 50-foot boat.

"Our sales were $500,000 last year; let's make $750,000 this year!" The U.S. has a cultural bias toward the more powerful, grandiose things: skyscrapers, lavish banquets, and especially big business. This logic pervades most advertising, marketing, and social training. You will find many business consultants immediately assume you hired them because you want *more*. More can be great, but more includes more responsibility, more work, and more debt. Ask yourself if the urge to grow your business is a personal motivation or simply a cultural bias you may have adopted without consciously considering your own Personal Definition of Success.

The number one reason for small business failures in the U.S. is rapid, unplanned growth. Often it is growth that forces businesses into cash jams, poor quality, and investments that never pay dividends; otherwise known as *growing broke*. It is also true that as the company grows, the role of the leader changes. Before your business grew, you may have been enjoying your time providing services and working with your customers. Now you are managing cash flow and focusing on marketing and training employees. As the owner of a burgeoning business, you may find yourself spending more time analyzing employee benefit packages than enjoying the benefits of being a business owner.

> When you start to develop your PDS, watch out for the most common assumption business owners make: bigger is better.

An engineer who was working on his own and making a good living, saw an opportunity to expand his firm and land larger jobs with bigger contracts. He partnered with two other engineers and grew the business. Over the years this once happy engineer became a frustrated manager. Why? Because what he loved about being an engineer was meeting with clients and finding the ideal engineering solution to their problems. Finding elegant solutions is what attracted him to engineering in the first place.

Growing the business without considering his PDS forced him to become a business manager — a role he quickly learned he didn't enjoy. Becoming a manager meant he had to acquire a whole new set of managerial and sales skills. He was rarely called upon to contribute engineering solutions anymore. Five years later this business leader dismantled the firm and went back to being a consulting engineer — a one-person show. A huge amount of time, energy, and money could have been saved, and a different Vision might very well have been realized, if he had included his PDS in his initial strategic decision-making process.

Business owners have many diverse goals for being in business, including:

- Create a full time job.
- Develop a company that can be passed along to their children.
- Develop a company that can be sold to the employees.
- Develop a company that can be sold to a competitor, vendor, or distributor.
- Develop a company to be franchised.
- Build a company that attracts the resources of outside investors.
- Build an investment that later provides passive income.
- Build a company that requires little or none of the owner's time to manage.
- Develop a personal reputation in the industry.
- Make a contribution to the community.

> Business owners have many diverse goals for being in business.

◈ Provide jobs for others in the community.

◈ Create a company that can go public.

◈ Provide an opportunity to develop leadership skills.

We are specifically talking about the actual owner because that is the person who is making the investment, taking the risks, and who will ultimately reap the consequences of the strategy (good, bad, or ugly). The owner is anyone with an equity stock position in a company; or in sole proprietorships and partnerships, those that are the registered owner(s) of the entity.

In a firm with several partners or principals it is important to appreciate the needs of each of them and include their perspectives when selecting the best Strategic Choices for the firm.

In a firm with several partners or principals it is important to appreciate the needs of each of them and include their perspectives when selecting the best Strategic Choices for the firm. In a publicly-held company, the owners are the stockholders, particularly the major stockholders. In some publicly-held companies the stockholders take the long view and are willing to maintain their investments even if the profits and stock growth are flat in the short-term. In other publicly-held companies profit is the major driver, from the stockholders perspective.

If you are managing a division of a major corporation or other large entity, you will want to incorporate the desires of that entity into your strategic decision-making process. An example of this is a firm that was involved in a roll-up. Our client who was once the owner, recognizes she is no longer the owner after the sale of her business, but remains the manager of her division. She, like any entrepreneur who has experienced the sale of the business to a larger firm, recognizes the need to appreciate the expectations of the new owners, in this case the corporation that purchased her firm, when a strategy is defined for the new division.

If you are a sole proprietor and actively doing business in a state with community property laws, then the business is considered community property between the registered owner and the spouse of the registered owner. These family-owned businesses need to take into consideration the needs of both partners in selecting the best Strategic Choices to lead the business (from this perspective).

When Should You Consider Including the PDS of Others in Your Business?

This question is important to contemplate as you envision your business from this perspective. You may want to incorporate the personal expectations of some other key people who are not currently owners. Some companies are small enough and close knit enough that every member is invited to put their PDS into the formula.

This can be a strong team-building exercise that promotes a team-oriented leadership style. An employee whose personal goals are important enough to be considered when developing the business strategy is likely to recognize the commitment the company is making to him, and do likewise. This can be very powerful if you are looking for employees to stay with the company for their entire careers; especially those employees you may be grooming for higher positions.

On the other hand, including too many people in your PDS perspective will dilute its value. If too many people contribute, it is difficult to summarize the results to mean anything more than simple fiscal security. Take the time to consider whose PDS should be taken into consideration in your strategic decision-making process.

The Business Owner's Values, Passions, and Ideals Fuel and Energize the Company

Persistence, more than talent, more than genius, is what results in success. The power that energizes the most successful business people to persist is the fact that they love what they do and do what they love. Incorporating your values and passion into your Vision for the business will energize and keep you going.

Personal Definitions of Success are always changing. How you defined success for yourself five or ten years ago may no longer hold true today, as in the case of a leader of a small law firm. The company had developed a unique specialty niche, which had resulted in a demand for their services nationally as well as

> You may want to incorporate the personal objectives of some other key people who are not currently owners.

regionally. When the principal was asked why the firm had chosen its niche, he replied that they really loved their work. When asked how he spent most of his time, he said he was on airplanes three days out of five. He didn't enjoy all the travel but he had always wanted to get national recognition for his work. He wasn't doing it for the money, he told me. He had plenty of money, and in fact had his retirement totally taken care of from other investments he had made outside his business. He admitted that his constant traveling had taken an unwanted toll on his marriage and family life, but he somehow felt compelled to maintain the business strategy he had been so enthusiastic about — 10 years ago!

> Consider what your motivations may be in the future, and anticipate your changing roles as the company evolves.

Values and priorities change with time. Five to ten years from now you may find yourself with a lack of motivation to continue in your current role. Consider what your motivations may be in the future, and anticipate your changing roles as the company evolves. If you are planning a change in your role in the company, the time to start anticipating that transition is now. Making decisions strategically means clarifying your personal motivations for running your business, and incorporating those motivations when choosing the best course for your business.

When you do not know where you are going, other people cannot help you get there. A business leader, like the captain of a ship, is dependent to a large degree on the crew. Without them, a successful voyage cannot be made. For the business leader, the crew consists of managers, employees, and trusted business advisers. In order to work effectively as a team with the crew, the owner must be totally clear about the destination, and communicate that motivation through the business' strategy.

Clarify Your Personal Definition of Success

Don't accept someone else's definition of success. And don't assume that an image of success that you have been pursuing out of habit is going to satisfy you. This is a rare opportunity for you to tell the truth about what is ultimately most important to you: profits, passive income, a team environment, building an empire, making a contribution to the community or to the planet, a quiet lifestyle, or whatever it is that fulfills your PDS. Take the time to summarize your PDS, envisioning yourself ten years in the future.

Begin by clarifying in general terms how you envision your life in the future. Focus your sights on a five-to ten-year horizon. Where you want to be five years from now is directly related to who you are now and what you expect your interests and needs to be then.

Clarifying the best direction to take the business based solely on the owner's PDS does not mean that you should, or have to, take that course. It does, however, greatly increase the business owner's ability to achieve personal, as well as professional, goals and to enjoy the workday that much more.

For the fourth time Good & Delicious looked at their Strategic Choices. The following Strategic Choices most directly meet the owners' needs and values:

> 2B. Strengthen superiority and reputation in designing successful QSR's (lighting, uniforms).
>
> 7B. Increase the number of sales through franchising.
>
> 5A. Dominate market share through mergers and acquisitions.
>
> 6A. Increase firm profits by focusing on soft drink products.

The following scenario describes Good & Delicious if it were to focus its investment of energy and resources in the Strategic Choices that best meet the Personal Definition of Success:

> *A sophisticated fast food management company that offers a franchise option to other investors and people interested in being store managers. As a fast food management company we purchase concepts and outlets and then turn them into profitable storefronts.*

Be sure that you
have truthfully been
looking from different
perspectives — and not
simply trying to force a
preconceived notion
through the process.

A word to the wise: if, as you proceed through the strategic decision-making process, you come up with the same Strategic Choices, and thus the same scenario, for each of the four perspectives, then you are either fooling yourself or you are the luckiest business owner on earth! Be sure that you have truthfully been looking from different perspectives — and not simply trying to force a preconceived notion through the process. Looking at *virtually anything* from different perspectives will present you with different pictures.

To be successful in the long-term, your strategy must be anchored in the business' Core Capabilities, limit the competition, be fueled by the owner's Personal Definition of Success, and meet forecasted market needs.

The factors that must be taken into consideration when developing a business strategy are large in number and varied in importance. They must be considered separately and in-depth before they can be combined to form a whole that is greater than the sum of its parts. Choosing four Strategic Choices from each of the four perspectives provides you with invaluable strategic insights that lead to the development of a compelling business strategy.

CHAPTER 7

Vision

••

If you think that your industry has seen all the innovations possible, check out some of the strategies that have come to our attention in 1999:

- ◈ How about a Vision for a new way to park cars? In response to a forecast for increased demand in parking and decreased availability of land worldwide, computer-run, mechanized garages that use forklift-like devices and rotating platforms to park your car are being commissioned in Europe and the U.S.

- ◈ In an industry that traditionally caters to the more affluent segment of society, how about a health spa for the not so rich? By excluding expensive, exotic space-intensive services, InSpa has opened a cost-effective health spa in a small space in Seattle, Washington. That's production efficiency.

- ◈ A Vision to provide quicker and better delivery of e-commerce from business to home has resulted in the teaming up of Airborne Express and the United States Postal Service.

◈ Venture catalysts are a new breed of animal. They are a visionary response to the need for business plans and consulting services by start-up firms looking for capital.

◈ How about a Vision for cleaning up litter. The "Adopt a Highway" campaign has helped to clean up our nation's roadways. Now that's visionary thinking.

◈ What is a unique way to sell expensive software to small business? Don't sell it, rent it. The coming wave in the distribution of high-end software is in rentals; just download straight from the Web.

◈ If you thought that Amazon.com was the only one to think of a new way to sell books, think again. What makes Third Place Books unique is that they combine new and used titles on the same shelves both online and in their stores. Traditionally, new and used books have been sold in separate shops — or at least in separate sections. Used books have a higher profit margin than new and thus represent a great opportunity for this entrepreneur with a Vision.

....

A Vision is a picture of what your business would become as a result of consistently investing in your selected and prioritized Strategic Choices.

Vision, according to *Webster's* dictionary, is "the ability to perceive something not actually visible, as through keen insight." In the case of a *business* Vision, keen insight is acquired by viewing your business through the four key perspectives and then finding where they overlap. A Vision is a picture of what your business would become as a result of consistently investing in your selected and prioritized Strategic Choices. Developing a business strategy is a visionary task. It deals with revealing previously unseen possibilities that result from combining Strategic Choices in new and unique ways. Our process of generating choices, viewing them from multiple perspectives, and creating scenarios, models the decision-making processes used intuitively by visionary leaders.

What is a visionary leader? A visionary is a person who can see possibilities that have never been seen before. Well-known visionaries of the 20th century include Martin Luther King, Mahatma Gandhi, John F. Kennedy, all of whom had a great impact on the sociopolitical landscape of our times. Business visionaries include Bill Gates and Lee Iacocca. Artistic visionaries include Pablo Picasso and Charlie Parker. These are people who have (had) the uncanny ability to see and articulate previously unrealized potentialities. They actually envision things that have not yet been seen. This ability to perceive the unseen comes naturally to some, but not to others. Fortunately, as far as business strategy is concerned, it is a capability that lends itself well to being communicated and learned. To communicate this skill we have broken the process down into easily manageable decisions. Many of those decisions come together in this chapter.

Up to now the concentration has been on generating viable Strategic Choices — the potential directions you could lead your business — that are based on the characteristics and capabilities that could set your business apart. Then the Strategic Choices were prioritized from each of the key perspectives and a scenario describing each perspective was developed.

Your business strategy is designed to position your company with a compelling Vision and an unfair advantage over the competition.

Stage One strategic decision-making moves the business leader through one of the toughest decisions you are responsible to make, the selection of your business strategy. Your business strategy is designed to position your company with a compelling Vision and an *unfair* advantage over the competition. This chapter focuses on locating the intersection of the four perspectives. The place where the four perspectives intersect points to a well founded, well-balanced business strategy, one that you have the confidence to implement. The overlapping circles in Figure 7.1 demonstrate how to find the intersection of the four perspectives.

Creating alternative scenarios for your business, as shown in the previous chapter, is an essential component of the visioning process — one that continues in this chapter. Considering alternative scenarios *before* you decide on a course to lead your business builds both clarity and confidence. Those people who see only one scenario, one option for their business tend to feel trapped and limited. Considering alternative scenarios, and projecting forward the subtle distinctions that separate them, is an important tool of the visionary leader. It requires a temporary suspension of judgment. We encourage the reader to proceed

FIGURE 7.1: The Intersection of the Four Perspectives

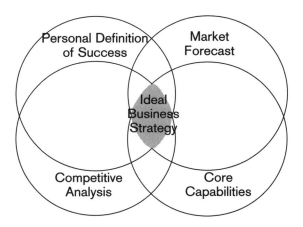

from a place of discovery, a sense of *not knowing*, that allows the unforeseen to emerge. Consider for a moment, that your Strategic Choices are the colored elements of glass within a kaleidoscope. Though the elements enclosed in the kaleidoscope don't change, every little turn of the kaleidoscope conjures up a totally unique, never before realized, image. Take the time to look at your business as if through a kaleidoscope. Consider the many alternative strategies you can come up with by combining your Strategic Choices in new ways.

A Business Strategy Is a Combination of Strategic Choices

The differentiators describe the nine basic ways in which businesses compete. Each of these ways are applied to your business to identify a minimum of nine Strategic Choices you can then combine to build a business strategy. How you combine and prioritize your Strategic Choices determines your business strategy and ultimately what your business will look like five to ten years from now. See Figure 7.2 for a visual representation of the development of a business strategy.

In the preceding chapters we have used many well-known businesses to exemplify the differentiators and how they work. Many of those examples like Microsoft, Starbucks, Nordstrom, Amazon.com, or Boeing use, or have used, Market Dominance as one of their top differentiators. The fact that these companies are so well known that they can be used as examples in a book with international readership is sufficient in itself to prove that they have invested heavily in Market Dominance by developing a brand, or dominating their respective markets. But even though we referred to these companies as being Market Dominant, Market Dominance was only one of the differentiators driving them.

One of the major advantages of using Market Dominance as a differentiator is to make your company or product's name synonymous with the product or service you provide. So when you think of computer operating systems, you think of Microsoft. When you think of Internet shopping you think of Amazon.com. When you think of automobiles you think of Ford. This "top-of-mind" awareness, which results from distinguishing a business on the basis of Market Dominance is very effective but, in and of itself, it is not enough. Boeing and Airbus compete with each other for market-share, however, they both use their second, third, and fourth differentiators to further distinguish themselves and attract customers. Boeing may compete with other airplane manufacturers on the basis of a manufacturing capability that

FIGURE 7.2: Business Strategy from Theory to Practice

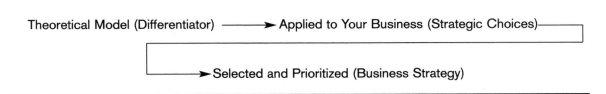

produces large, long-distance, reliable, airplanes efficiently and on schedule. Airbus may compete on the basis of their ability to offer a high quality, customized product, at a subsidized price.

Market Dominance must be combinedwith other differentiators such as Market Responsive, Product Superiority, or unique Method of Sale. For example, Microsoft began with an expertise in MS-DOS that led to the development of Windows-based products. They used that Superiority in computer operating systems to fuel growth and achieve market domination. At the same time they continued to invest heavily in Technology, and to fulfill the entire needs of the personal computer market.

Although it will continue to change, Microsoft's business strategy was probably composed of:

- ◆ Market Dominance
- ◆ Product Superiority
- ◆ Technology
- ◆ Market Responsive

> Strategic Choices are the building blocks of business strategy; to create a strategy you select, combine, and prioritize your Strategic Choices.

Strategic Choices are the building blocks of business strategy; to create a strategy you select, combine, and prioritize your Strategic Choices. The way in which you combine and prioritize your Strategic Choices, and the percentage of your resources that are invested in each of them, determines your strategy, who you compete directly with, and how your market recognizes you. In fact the percentage of resources actually invested in each of your Strategic Choices determines their true prioritization.

The way in which you combine and prioritize the Strategic Choices impacts the direction of your business. The Nordstrom brothers started as retailers of expensive imported shoes. Their expertise was enhanced by a commitment to exceptional customer service. After they experienced success with this strategy they broadened the business to include a full line of retail products (Market Responsive), all the while retaining their focus on customer service. In the early 1990s their strategy again changed. They went public and started opening stores all over the U.S. (Market Dominance). Resources that were previously used to maintain superiority in exceptional customer service were diverted to fuel growth.

Ten years ago Nordstrom's Strategic Choices probably stacked up like this:

- *Method of Sale*: A strong focus on extraordinary customer service.

- *Market Responsive*: Respond to the needs of retail shoppers with fashionable products.

- *Human Resources*: Maintain excellent staff.

- *Short-Term Profit*: Price inventory at a premium.

Who was attracted to Nordstrom as a result of this strategy? Affluent shoppers who wanted high quality, designer-label clothing, and a level of customer service that could be called legendary.

However, at the time of this writing Nordstrom no longer seems to be providing the customer service that, at one time, gave them a clear competitive advantage. In 1999, for the first time in over ten years, they did not make the list of top ten U.S. companies in customer service. The mythology surrounding their exceptional customer service no longer abounds. The "I'd rather be shopping at Nordstrom" license plates have become collector's items. For many, Nordstrom is now simply another large chain of high-end retail merchandise.

The building blocks of their present strategy appear to be:

- *Market Dominance*: Establish a national presence.

- *Market Responsive*: Respond to the needs of retail shoppers with fashionable products.

- *Production Efficiency*: Standardize procedures and systems to provide consistent service throughout the chain.

- *Method of Sale*: A strong focus on customer service.

Who is attracted to Nordstrom as a result of this strategy? The middle class shopper who frequents malls looking for brand name apparel and is attracted to Nordstrom because of their past reputation for customer service.

Did Nordstrom make a mistake by shifting their direction from Customer Service to Market Dominance? The answer is no, not necessarily. If Nordstrom's management chose to change the company's direction as the result of forecasted market needs, an analysis of the competition, an understanding of company strengths and the owner's long-term personal goals, then it may very well have been the right decision. If, however, they chose to grow *while at the same time* maintain the same level of legendary customer service, then they may have made an error in judgment. Whereas before Nordstrom had an "open return" policy, their national expansion necessitated the enforcement of posted return policies. Staff needed to be brought in quickly, training priorities changed. Executive attention and resources quite naturally became focused on the issues of growth, selecting building sites, approving building plans, and watching stock prices.

The point is that it is not possible for a business to be driven *equally* by two differentiators, in this case Market Dominance and Method of Sale. One will always take precedence over the other. There is a huge difference in the following strategies: "Our top priority is to maintain the highest customer service standards and expand when the opportunity permits" and "We will expand and do our best to continue providing great service." The first tenet of business strategy: *you cannot be all things to all people* comes in to play more and more as you proceed through strategic decision-making. The markets attracted to each of Nordstrom's strategies, though not entirely mutually exclusive, are dissimilar and require different systems and priorities to accommodate.

Whether it was planned or not, we do not know, but when Market Dominance got moved to the top of Nordstrom's Strategic Choices, Method of Sale (in the form of extraordinary customer service), was simply displaced and moved to a lower

....

It is not possible for a business to be driven equally by two differentiators.

position. The impact is dramatic. The "top-of-mind" awareness, which results from distinguishing a business on the basis of Market Dominance is very effective but like every other Strategic Choice, rising to the top means displacing some other strategy.

All of the Strategic Choices work some of the time and none of the Strategic Choices work all of the time. The key to making business strategy work for you is to make each of your strategic decisions consciously and with intention, having done your due diligence to anticipate the potential impact a change in priorities will have on your current clients and future prospects.

Top Four Strategic Choices

Although every business competes, to some degree, using each of the differentiators, it is generally the four highest-priority differentiators and their associated Strategic Choices that do the majority of the work distinguishing one business from the other.

....

It is essential to allocate resources consistently with your selected and prioritized Strategic Choices.

Historically, strategic decision-making has shown that most businesses cannot focus on operationalizing more than four or five Strategic Choices successfully at one time. It is essential to allocate resources consistently with your selected and prioritized Strategic Choices. This means that it is generally best to allocate the highest percentage of resources to your number one Strategic Choice. The second highest percentage goes to your second level Strategic Choice, and so on. Choose and prioritize only your four top Strategic Choices. The remaining differentiators will fall into place to support your strategy quite naturally.

Choosing the four most important Strategic Choices can be a formidable-looking task. Beware of these common mistakes:

- ⬥ Combining several Strategic Choices into one.
- ⬥ Excluding your number one Strategic Choice because it is already a well-established priority.
- ⬥ Making the third and fourth positions equal.

Combining Several Strategic Choices Into One

In Chapter 5 we presented the list of Strategic Choices generated by Good & Delicious. They developed several Strategic Choices for many of the differentiators. It is not at all unusual for a business to have two to four Strategic Choices for each differentiator on their master list.

Applied Business Solutions, Inc. identified the following Market Responsive choices in our own strategic decision-making in 1997:

1. Respond to the needs of, and develop strategic decision-making products specifically for, small business owners.

2. Respond to the needs of, and develop strategic decision-making products for, large CPA firms.

3. Respond to the needs of, and develop strategic decision-making products specifically for, professional service firms.

Your strategy will lose much of its power if you try to combine Strategic Choices to make your decision-making easier.

Like our clients, we had to resist the temptation to combine each of these distinctly different but sometimes overlapping Strategic Choices. It would have been a mistake to try to respond to the needs of, and develop strategic decision-making products for, *large CPA's, small business owners, and professional service firms.* The power gained by naming a specific market, surveying their needs, and focusing your resources on developing products or services to meet those needs, will be lost if that named target market is too broad. Your strategy will lose much of its power if you try to combine Strategic Choices to make your decision-making easier.

For example, what do you think when you pass a restaurant sign that reads: "We specialize in Chinese and Italian food"? The term *specialize* seems to be used very loosely. In fact they don't seem like specialists at all. In a pinch, you might have lunch there, but your expectations would not be high, nor would you be willing to order if the prices were above average. It is common to be wary of businesses that claim to be experts in a long list of services and products. If you try to take short cuts by combining

Strategic Choices into one all-inclusive Strategic Choice, you can no longer expect it to function effectively in clarifying your strategic priorities.

Excluding Your Number One Strategic Choice because It Is Already a Well-Established Priority

As you continue the process of narrowing down your Strategic Choices to four it is easy to make the mistake of excluding your most important Strategic Choice if it is already a well-established priority. Nordstrom may have believed that their commitment to exceptional customer service was a "given" and that they could refocus their resource allocation without negatively impacting their ability to provide it. Each characteristic or capability you use to set your business apart must be aligned with a differentiator and then prioritized according to its importance.

Strategic Choices are the engines that propel your company toward fulfillment of your Vision. Do not make the mistake of assuming that a Strategic Choice from the past (or present) will continue to power your business. Like all engines, your Strategic Choices need to be fueled and maintained or they will stop working. How much fuel and maintenance a particular Strategic Choice receives is directly dependent on its level of prioritization. To be a priority, and receive its fair share of resources, remember to include the number one characteristic that sets your business apart, in your final selection of Strategic Choices.

Making the Third and Fourth Positions Equal

The opportunity for some really unique strategic positioning comes with your third and fourth Strategic Choices. Beware of the temptation to give them equal priority. For most business leaders the top two Strategic Choices are fairly obvious. The subtleties of business strategy, the capabilities that often really serve to make a business unique, can be designed and communicated by the Strategic Choices occupying the third and fourth positions.

> Each characteristic or capability you use to set your business apart must be aligned with a differentiator and then prioritized according to its importance.

An example of this is the industry of business consulting; at Applied Business Solutions, Inc.

- ✦ Our number one Strategic Choice is Product Superiority: We are specialists in strategic planning/decision-making tools.

- ✦ Our number two Strategic Choice is Production Efficiency: Strategic planning retreats and seminars.

- ✦ Our number three Strategic Choice is Method of Sales: Products like strategic decision-making books, work-books, and CD-ROMs that increase our reputation and introduce companies to our services.

- ✦ Our number four Strategic Choice is Method of Distribution: Create strategic alliances with major accounts that license and resell our products.

Our expertise in strategic decision-making separates us from 99 percent of all other business consultants. Even so, we would still be competing with thousands of consultants that specialize in strategic planning if it weren't for our third and fourth Strategic Choices. Our number two Strategic Choice, seminars and retreats, distinguishes us further but not significantly so. However, developing user-friendly resources such as books and CD-ROMs increases our visibility tremendously, fills a market need, and supports our top two choices. Creating strategic alliances with major accounts, like large CPA firms, to license our strategic decision-making model, has served as both a Method of Sale *and* Distribution. Many of our competitors utilize Strategic Choices that are similar to our top two. But our last two choices are what really refined our business strategy and, combined with the top two, make us unique.

It is important to recognize the differences in priority of your Strategic Choices. Each has its rightful place, its level of importance in your strategy. Avoid the tendency to create *equal* Strategic Choices — choices that supposedly occupy the same level of priority. No two Strategic Choices can be given the same priority.

....

Avoid the tendency to create equal Strategic Choices – choices that supposedly occupy the same level of priority.

Vision

An effective business strategy takes into account forecasted market needs, what the competition is doing, the business' Core Capabilities, and the owner's Personal Definition of Success. Review the Strategic Choices you selected to meet each of these perspectives. The Strategic Choices that appear most frequently overall, and in the highest priority positions, are the ones that should be given the greatest consideration in your final selection and prioritization.

Check out the following guidelines for selecting and prioritizing your final four Strategic Choices.

- Emphasize Strategic Choices that appear most often from the four perspectives.

- Specific business circumstances may impact the importance you give to one or two perspectives over the others.

- Select one Strategic Choice from each of the four perspectives.

- Create alternative scenarios.

Emphasize Strategic Choices that Appear Most Often from the Four Perspectives

If the same Strategic Choice appeared three times when viewing your business from the four perspectives, it means that choice fulfills the requirements set by three of the four perspectives. This is good. That Strategic Choice should be given very strong consideration in your final selection. However, using only the number of times a Strategic Choice appeared, or the level of priority the Strategic Choice was given can mistakenly turn this into a mathematical exercise.

Just because a Strategic Choice appears often doesn't mean you have to give it top billing. If in fact you have one Strategic Choice that appeared four times it still does not necessarily make it your business' top Strategic Choice. This is *not* a mathematical exercise! Use the frequency at which a Strategic Choice showed up, and the level of priority you gave it, simply *as a guideline*. Use your common business sense and the insights you gain by creating alternate scenarios to guide your final decision.

Specific Business Circumstances May Impact the Importance You Give to One or Two Perspectives

Based on your circumstances, one or two of the perspectives may carry more weight for you. The Competitive Analysis may be more important to you than the other perspectives if you are focused heavily on market domination. The owner's PDS may have more importance if you are a small family-owned company. Your Core Capabilities may carry more significance in your decision-making if you are severely limited in investment capital. And when you are in an industry that is forced to change because of forecasted market needs, the requirements dictated by those changes will increase in importance. Each of the perspectives has equal value in theory, but in practice weigh them proportionately to your particular circumstances.

Select One Strategic Choice from Each of the Four Perspectives

When selecting your final strategy it makes good sense, though it is not essential, to choose a Strategic Choice from each of the four perspectives. Selecting at least one Strategic Choice from each of the four perspectives ensures you are selecting a business strategy that builds on your current Core Capabilities. It also takes into account the owner's PDS, prepares the company for the forecasted market, and positions you to compete on a different basis than the majority of your competitors. A well-balanced strategy meets the needs of each of the four perspectives.

Create Alternative Scenarios

To facilitate this decision it is helpful to create and consider alternative scenarios by combining your Strategic Choices in several different ways. We will continue using Good & Delicious as an

....

When selecting your final strategy it makes good sense, though it is not essential, to choose a Strategic Choice from each of the four perspectives.

example. The intersection of their four perspectives revealed that Strategic Choices 1B, 4A, and 6A all showed up twice. In this instance no single Strategic Choice stood out head and shoulders above the rest.

They began looking at how these Strategic Choices might work together. Accordingly they took 1B, 4A, and 6A, added a Strategic Choice that had only appeared once, and started developing scenarios.

Scenario 1

6A. Increase firm profits by focusing on soft drink products.

4A. Strengthen and retain HR through profit sharing and incentives.

2A. Strengthen superiority and reputation in quality customer service.

1B. Respond to the needs of the landlords/developers.

The (abbreviated) Vision for a business using this strategy would look like:

Our focus is on developing a unique line of soft drinks that are delicious as well as healthy, and offer us the greatest margins and return on investment. Our investment in Human Resources creates a strong bond with our customer base that knows us for our friendly and exceptional customer service. Developers and commercial landlords know us as the company that can generate significant profits from a small facility.

The management team considered this a plausible scenario but was not totally satisfied, so they developed another one.

Scenario 2

5A. Dominate the market through mergers and acquisitions.

1B. Respond to the needs of landlords/developers.

2A. Strengthen superiority and reputation in quality customer service.

4A. Strengthen and retain HR through profit sharing and incentives.

The (abbreviated) Vision for a business using this strategy would look like:

By merging with and acquiring other fast food restaurant chains we dominate the fast food market starting in the Northeastern U.S. This enables us to respond to the needs of developers with a full menu of fast food outlet solutions. Our outlets are known for their excellent service. Our employees are the keys to our continued success and we reward them accordingly. Maximizing our Human Resources through profit sharing and incentives give us an edge over our competition.

Business strategy is about setting priorities. It is clear that the priorities a business must set to achieve Scenario 1 would be different than the priorities it would set to achieve Scenario 2. The management team of Good & Delicious recombined their Strategic Choices several more times until they were satisfied with the following:

1B. Respond to the needs of the landlords/developers.

6A. Increase firm profits by focusing on soft drink products.

5A. Dominate market share through mergers and acquisitions.

2A. Strengthen superiority and reputation in quality customer service.

The management teams' Vision based on consistently investing in the above four, selected and prioritized, Strategic Choices follows:

Good & Delicious responds to the food-court needs of mall owners and developers. Our ability to help them find the right solutions

······················

Business strategy is
about setting priorities.

positions us as their preferred fast-food restaurant providers. Our willingness to take on new venues and offerings, products or concepts motivates developers to return to us year after year, project after project to fulfill their food-court requirements.

Good & Delicious is a highly profitable company. We focus on developing a unique line of soft drinks that are delicious as well as healthy, and offer us the greatest margins and return on investment. This provides us with the operating capital we need to grow.

Our Vision is to lead the fast-food industry in the next ten years. We plan to attain this growth through acquisitions and mergers. The profits from our soft drinks enable us to purchase our smaller competitors. When the need arises, and whenever a great opportunity presents itself, we will merge with same size or larger fast-food restaurants interested in collaborating with our strategy.

Good & Delicious is known for its outstanding commitment to quality service and foods. Our customers love the way our products taste, and feel safe that the products they purchase for their and their children's consumption are fresh, clean, and nutritious. We are the benchmark against which quality is measured by the food-court service industry

> A business Vision is an
> internal communication
> tool designed to
> summarize and set
> forth the priorities
> set by the selected
> strategy.

Before finalizing your strategy it is a good idea to create and envision several alternative scenarios to get a feel for how a reshuffling of your Strategic Choices can result in a very different Vision. Play around with different combinations until you come up with one that meets the suggested guidelines and simply feels right.

Build Your Business Vision

A *business* Vision is an internal communication tool designed to summarize and set forth the priorities set by the selected strategy. It is a visual description, a picture of what your business will become as a result of consistently investing in your prioritized Strategic Choices. It is the destination you aim your business towards.

Clearly communicate your selected and prioritized Strategic Choices in your Vision statement. Write one short paragraph illustrating each of your final four Strategic Choices. The Vision is written in present tense. Some companies find it helpful to include information about why a Strategic Choice was selected, the values it represents, or the benefits to the company's clients. No matter what you choose to include in your Vision statement be sure that your Strategic Choices are clearly defined and discussed in priority order.

Examples of Vision statements:

XYZ's Strategy

Market Responsive: Focus on employers with over 100 employees in Missoula County.

Product Superiority: Training programs that promote staff development.

Method of Sales: Certificate programs.

Technology: Distance learning programs.

XYZ's Vision

We respond to the training needs of organizations with over 100 employees in Missoula County. We identify and develop relationships with our well-defined target market. Our annual survey process allows us to stay abreast of their needs and proactively develop training programs which meet their expectations. Our commitment to our clients demonstrates we know, understand, and care about these organizations.

Our internal training programs ensure that each employee has the opportunity to develop to their full potential, and result in strong employee retention rates for each of our clients. In addition, our strategic alliance with Staff Service allows us to offer temporary staffing and placement services to ensure our clients have the people they need to get their work done. We help our customers train their current workforce and provide trained workers to meet their needs with an up-to-date and wide breadth of training options.

> No matter what you choose to include in your Vision statement be sure that your Strategic Choices are clearly defined and included in priority order.

Our specialized certification programs are a strong asset, both to the business community and to the community college. These programs set the standards of a qualified, trained workforce of today and the future.

Our distance learning programs make learning more accessible to the developing workforce. We have a reputation as the training resource of choice, both before and after you are employed. We contribute to the economic development of our community and help prepare each future job candidate to be the ideal solution for our client's needs.

ABC's Strategy

Human Resources: Employee-owned enterprise.

Market Responsive: International companies who have ongoing publishing needs and focus on large documents.

Production Efficiency: Work on projects requiring repeat editions or re-purposing.

Product Superiority: Translations into foreign languages.

ABC's Vision

ABC is a medium sized, employee-owned, service company. Our employees' commitment to the company and the company's commitment to its employees provide us with the staff and resources necessary to compete in the marketplace. We focus on building a strong, well-trained, team that values personal advancement and balance with our family and community.

Our commitment to respond to the needs of international companies who have ongoing publishing needs and work with large documents allows us to better understand their requirements and develop new services to meet their needs.

We build strong and lasting relationships with clients who produce repeat editions. These ongoing contracts provide the company with the cash flow and consistency to support the development of staff and investment in tools that promote our production efficiency. Our ability to re-purpose our client's materials challenges us to find solutions that work in multiple formats and meet our client's needs at significant savings.

Our expertise in translation will assist our clients in building their international business. We are their preferred choice because we can translate and produce their documents (in all mediums) in up to 24 different languages.

> Selecting a strategy and developing your Vision results in clearly defined strategic priorities for your company.

Selecting a strategy and developing your Vision results in clearly defined strategic priorities for your company. This strategic positioning decision is the most important job of a visionary business leader. After selecting a strategy, the next step is to write a compelling Vision statement that summarizes your decisions.

Your Vision Statement Is a Summary of the Decisions Made in Stage One

Communicate your decisions in a way that motivates others to honor the priorities set forth in your Vision. The business Vision is the answer to what are your strategic priorities, where the business is going, and why you have decided on this focus. Your Vision is a very powerful communication tool.

All partners, employees, and investors should understand the direction you plan to take the company. It is extremely useful to provide these people with your Vision, as it summarizes your business strategy as well as your expectations for investing resources consistently in the characteristics and capabilities that give your business its competitive advantage. When people know where you are going they are more able to help you get there.

For example, when you are buying marketing expertise (copy writing, identity, brochure, or advertising packages) the service firm working with you on this project will need to know your Vision. When you want to hire additional staff they will want to know your Vision. Visions are also helpful to share with your professional advisers, networks, and vendors. Use your Vision as a tool to let others know where your business is heading.

Your Vision Motivates You and Others

The most efficient way to keep a boat on course is to pick a landmark on the horizon and steer toward it. Your Vision is the landmark that you will steer for. You use it as a quick and consistent reference when making important operational decisions. Your Vision acts like a magnet drawing you toward, and reminding you of, the destination that you have chosen. It will also attract others to invest in your business, suggest creative new opportunities, and purchase your products and services.

Your Vision Provides an Immediate Clarification of Business Priorities.

Your Vision statement lets everyone in the business know what your priorities are. This enables your employees to work and make decisions consistent with those priorities. This reduces the need to micro-manage and empowers your entire team.

Vision Tag Line

Your Vision tag line is a five-word summary of your Vision and is often called your marketing slogan. Whereas the more descriptive Vision statement is often considered an internal document, the Vision tag line is a slogan that can be used in marketing and with external communications pieces. It represents your number one Strategic Choice and cleverly informs your market of your top priority differentiator.

Vision and Mission

A Vision, as previously described, is a motivational, internal, document that records your strategic decisions and core purpose

> Your Vision statement lets everyone in the business know what your priorities are.

for being in business, and helps everyone in the company stay focused on your priorities and where your business is headed.

A Mission statement, in contrast, is a concise answer to the question, "What does your company do?" It states who your target market is, what your priority services are, and how you provide those services in a way that distinguishes you from your competitors. It is a public statement that is designed to attract your target market by having them recognize themselves and their needs, as well as the benefits of using your company to attain those needs.

The end of Chapter 7 also marks the end of Stage One: Strategy. Stage One started with generating a comprehensive list of Strategic Choices and it concluded with the selection of the final four Strategic Choices that were combined and prioritized to form a viable and compelling business strategy. Those choices form the basis of a business Vision, the result of Stage One. The next Chapter begins Stage Two of the process: Focus.

In Stage Two we prepare the business leader to develop a Mission. The focus is on the decisions that define your target market and prioritize your products and services.

Focus

· ·

· · · · · · · · · · · · · · · · · ·

The result of making
Stage Two decisions is
summarized in your
Mission statement.

Your Vision describes your destination. Focus enables you to find it. This chapter presents useful guidelines for determining *which* market will be most attracted to your company's strategy, and *which* products and services your target market will most want to purchase. The result of making Stage Two decisions is summarized in your Mission statement.

A new car dealer realizes that 40 percent of the time, when a past customer walks in the door, he or she drives out with a new car. This is in comparison to the percentage of sales made to new customers, which are around 20 percent. After discovering this the car dealer knows that his target market is a repeat customer. He has the receptionist pre-screen all callers and customers to determine if they are past customers and instructs his salespeople to attend to those prospects first. In addition he sends out a promotional offering for a free oil change to customers who purchased a car from him within the last five years. While the service is being performed, the customer gets a tour of the showroom.

A target market is the clearly defined group of customers and prospects that are attracted to the specific characteristics and capabilities leveraged by your business strategy. Use your Vision to gain a tighter focus and new insights into your ideal target market and priority products and services. Your business strategy and its resulting Vision determine who your target market is. Defining your business strategy clarifies very specifically which customers, products and services you should focus your business on. Focusing in on your Vision greatly increases momentum.

....

Use your Vision to gain a tighter focus and new insights into your ideal target market and priority products and services.

Two different landscape architect firms will be used to demonstrate how two businesses from the same industry, each with a different Vision, attract different target markets.

Firm A's business strategy is composed of the following prioritized Strategic Choices:

- *Product Superiority*: Specialize in design of community open-spaces and campuses.

- *Method of Sale*: The firm's principals sit on the boards of many of the civic and community-minded organizations in which they are actively engaged.

- *Human Resources*: Principals with award winning design portfolios.

- *Short-Term Profit*: Operate individual design studios as profit centers.

Based on their business strategy, firm A was able to define their target market. They identified it as community leaders that have the interest and the funds to invest in landmark public spaces. Their target market likes to work with people they know personally, and they are more interested in the quality of results than the pricing. Their selected target market and prioritized services/products are summarized in their Mission.

Firm A's Mission
We specialize in working closely with community leaders who are committed to leaving a legacy for generations to come. Our team of award-winning architects design community parks and campuses.

Firm B's strategy is composed of the following prioritized Strategic Choices:

- ◈ *Production Efficiency*: Easily adapted landscape design templates for public spaces in housing developments.

- ◈ *Market Responsive*: A full range of landscape design solutions for private developers.

- ◈ *Technology*: Online pricing.

- ◈ *Product Superiority*: Recreational areas.

Based on their business strategy, firm B was able to define their target market as the busy developers of planned residential communities who want to sub-out all their landscape design to a single firm. They want fast, inexpensive, and dependable service. Their selected target market and prioritized services/products are summarized in their Mission.

Firm B's Mission

Our full range of standardized landscape design solutions fills all the needs of community developers. Online selection and pricing makes us the preferred partner for developers of recreational areas looking for cost-effective landscape designs.

Both firms are in the same industry, landscape design, but because they have chosen very different strategies they have completely different target markets as well as a different set of services. Firm A would be wasting their time and money marketing to the customers that need what Firm B has to offer, and vice versa. To maximize resources, and sail the most direct course to your Vision, it is essential to focus on the customers and products or services best matched to your Vision.

These distinctions are equally, if not more important in situations where the business strategies are more similar than in the example just described. For example, stores offering virtually identical inventory like True Value Hardware and Home Depot. There will always be customers looking for the least expensive solutions just as there are always customers for whom convenience or service counts most. Some markets are

....

There will always be customers looking for the least expensive solutions just as there are always customers for whom convenience or service counts most.

willing to pay for full service, others make their buying decisions based on the personality of the staff, and so on. The purpose of this chapter is to provide you with tools for identifying the target market best suited to your business strategy. Your strategy not only defines who you are, but also who your target market is.

Navigating Toward Your Vision

Once the Captain of a ship decides to sail from San Francisco to Hawaii, has she finished her navigational calculations? No, in order to chart a course she must first figure out the exact coordinates of her destination, the intersection of latitude and longitude.

....

The intersection of your primary customers and primary products provides essential insights into customer prospecting, customer retention, and product development.

The business leader is also looking for the intersection of two coordinates. However, instead of latitude and longitude you are seeking the intersection of your primary customers (target market) and your primary products or services. Locating the intersection of these two coordinates is the central decision in Stage Two strategic decision-making, and an important step in turning your Vision into Action. The intersection of your primary customers and primary products provides essential insights into customer prospecting, customer retention, and product development. The intersection of your primary customers with your primary services is the target to focus your sights on. Figure 8.1 illustrates how to focus in on your Vision.

A newly defined strategy and resulting Vision means that your business has identified a new destination. Even if you have chosen to only make a small course correction, it is important to establish the exact coordinates of your new destination. Second-level strategic decision-making centers on identifying the customers and products or services that create the greatest momentum toward your Vision. The key is to use your Vision like a lens, to see and analyze your historical sales data in ways you may never have before.

Use your Vision to drive the selection of your target market. For instance, building your business so you can franchise it in the

FIGURE 8.1: Locating Two Coordinates

next five years is a very different Vision than if you plan to build a reputation for high quality, exclusive, high-priced products. Your Vision drives your selection of your highest priority products or services and who your target market should be. A structured and rigorous investigation determines *which* products or services to sell to *which* customers in order to achieve your Vision. The results of making Stage Two decisions are summarized in your Mission statement.

Why is focusing tightly on your target market so important? The answer is, for several reasons. To begin with, most businesses have limited resources. Also, some of your customers, products, and services will give you more momentum toward your Vision. Focusing in on your target market enables you to prioritize your marketing and employee efforts.

Your Vision drives your selection of your highest priority products or services and who your target market should be.

Most Businesses Have Limited Resources

Simply put, no business can afford to waste valuable time, energy, and money bringing products to an unresponsive market or bringing unwanted products to their customers. It is essential to establish with precision *which* customers to target and *which* products or services to offer. Focusing in on your target market and primary products enables you to maximize marketing dollars, streamline marketing initiatives, and make the best use of your production capabilities.

Identify Which Customers and Which Products or Services Provide You with the Most Momentum

Apply the 80/20 rule (also known as the Parieto Principle), to identify the 20 percent of your products or services that provide you with 80 percent of the momentum toward your Vision. Alfredo Parieto, an 18th century economist, uncovered an amazingly persistent principle that helps us appreciate the importance of prioritizing. In his original study he measured the distribution of wealth in Italy. He found that 80 percent of the wealth was held by 20 percent of the people. He later realized that his (so-called) 80/20 rule could be extended to many areas in life. For example, 20 percent of your customers purchase 80 percent of your products. Twenty percent of your people earn 80 percent of your payroll. Twenty percent of your services produce 80 percent of your profits and on and on.

Your biggest customer is not necessarily the type of customer you should target. Many companies make mistaken assumptions about who their primary customers are. Most companies decide who their major customers are based on the size and profitability of the account. For the small business leader, winning a high volume customer seems like a stroke of luck. Instantly 80 percent of your revenues come from one source. However, once that source recognizes your dependence on them they often continue to make bigger and bigger demands. These demands may include increasing capacity and staffing, reducing margins, and product development. Becoming a captive provider to a major customer can debilitate a company's other client relationships and destabilize the company's future.

A small training company won an account with a major corporation. In order to win this account they had to reduce their prices and promise to increase their capacity. The focus on this

> Your biggest customer is not necessarily the type of customer you should target.

WORKSHEET 7: Applying the 80/20 Rule to Your Company

What do you know already about how the 80/20 rule applies to your company?

_____

_____

What is the value for you of focusing on the 20 percent of customers that provide you 80 percent of the momentum toward your Vision?

_____

_____

Does your largest account provide you with the most momentum toward your Vision?

_____

_____

Does your most profitable account provide you with the most momentum toward your Vision?

_____

_____

one account reduced their customer service to their other clients. Ultimately their other more profitable and less demanding clients started looking for other suppliers. As a result the company became dependent on their big account and found themselves working harder, stretching their resources, and making less money while not having the time and energy to go find other accounts.

Strategic decision-making helped this firm address this predicament and change its thinking to see that bigger clients are not necessarily the best clients. The best clients provide the most momentum towards your long-term Vision. The management team then agreed to find at least five new clients that equaled their fixed operating costs and to move their number one client into a maintenance position. The result is they were back at the helm and no longer dependent on the one main client.

The purpose of this chapter is to challenge you to identify and increase the 20 percent of your customers that provide you with 80 percent of the momentum towards your Vision. By focusing your energies on increasing that 20 percent by just 1 percent you will be far further ahead than by focusing your energies on increasing the other 80 percent by 10 percent.

A department store could take a large leap toward turning its Vision into Action by alerting their staff to their product priorities. Their strategy is to expand the number of sales to each customer. They learned that their greatest margins come from smaller accessories purchased to compliment larger purchases. With this information firmly in mind they focused their promotions and sales training to ensure that each customer is invited to accessorize their purchases. In addition, they discovered that men between the ages of 25 and 45 are more likely to buy additional accessories than other types of customers. Armed with this information they will be able to add additional incentives to attract and capture that market.

A small professional service firm has about 40 clients who they analyzed to identify their "ideal target market." In Stage Two of their strategic decision-making they created a profile of their target market and project type. Interestingly enough they already had 12 clients that perfectly matched their Vision. The funny thing was that nine of those clients had not been traditionally seen as high priority clients for the firm because the projects they required were smaller, lower visibility, and required less executive management. However, these clients will provide the maximum momentum for the company to achieve its Vision. With this insight in mind the project managers took a new interest in these clients and the marketing department was able to refocus their efforts to find more clients that matched the profile.

> By focusing your energies on increasing that 20 percent by just 1 percent you will be far further ahead than by focusing your energies on increasing the other 80 percent by 10 percent.

Keeping track of *which* products or services give you the best return on your resources means more than simply taking inventory. It involves analyzing past sales, looking for common characteristics, and identifying which products or customer groups provide you with the most momentum toward your Vision.

Prioritize Your Marketing and Employee Efforts

All businesses must make choices. Should you respond to this proposal or that proposal? Should you invest in this work today or invest your time marketing for tomorrow? Should you expand your expertise in this area or that area? Choices are a part of daily decision-making. Most businesses are moving so fast that employees on all levels are forced to answer the *which* question many times in each workday. Every employee should understand your business priorities and be in a position to make decisions based on those priorities.

> Most businesses are moving so fast that employees on all levels are forced to answer the which question many times in each workday.

The Stage Two decisions are decided by the business leader or management team and then communicated clearly so everyone in the company can consistently make the right decisions, and your priority customers are provided with a consistently high level of service. Once you identify the primary services and customers that best match your strategy, you can communicate your priorities to the rest of your team, your marketing support people, and your priority customers.

Answering the second level strategic question helps you prioritize your company's responses to your customers. Every one of your employees who deals with customers needs to know who your highest priority customers are so they receive the first and best service. Every one of your employees that is involved in the production or distribution of your services/products should know which of your products are the highest priority to produce, distribute, and sell. Identifying the characteristics of your target market facilitates your crew's ability to recognize your priority customers immediately when they walk in the door or make any kind of inquiry into your product/service offering. Once your crew understands which 20 percent of your business makes the greatest impact toward your Vision, everyone can focus on identifying, serving, and expanding those areas.

Is everyone you provide service to in your target market? Probably not; many businesses already have some customers who represent their target market and even more customers that come to them for a host of other reasons. The exact percentages of one to the other differ with each business. As you adjust your business' course, you will want to focus on getting more and more of your target market and less and less of the kind of business that you are not trying to attract. This is important because a lot of resources that could be spent on getting more of the business that powers you towards your Vision is wasted on business you don't really want. Do not stop servicing that default business, just work toward replacing it with customers from your target market.

Understandably this concept is a little challenging to put into action. Most businesses are currently operating with 20 percent of their revenue coming from the *right* types of products, services, or customers. The rest of the income comes from what are commonly called "opportunity" sales. The 20 percent of your work that gives you direct momentum toward your Vision is the *right* work. The other 80 percent is "opportunity" business.

Why are we business leaders reluctant to prioritize customers? Because we know every customer is important — no matter how small the sale is, or how many resources are required to service that account. We appreciate that the 80 percent opportunity sales often pay the rent. Opportunity sales often provide the consistent cash flow a law firm needs between big cases, or an author needs between big novels, or a caterer needs to tide them over between holidays. They also represent a significant cost.

Over the last decade the business economy has been booming and many businesses feel they have been forced to grow just to "keep up with the market." Unfortunately as businesses grow they tend to hang onto the deadweight (customers *or* products) that no longer provides much value. It is a vicious cycle. You hire staff to service clients and then you need to find additional work to keep the staff busy. Instead of maintaining the staff at a

> Most businesses are currently operating with 20 percent of their revenue coming from the right types of products, services, or customers.

manageable (read profitable) size and focusing their efforts on your target market, you hire staff to try to cover all the work that the world creates. This puts a tremendous strain on your resources, making it difficult to pursue the kind of work best matched to your business strategy.

For example, in a mid-size travel agency, all the agents have their own accounts, and the needs of those accounts are naturally addressed or prioritized by the order in which they come in, or based on the personal relationship of the agent with the account. However, after a strategic analysis it became clear that 80 percent of the travel this agency sold was to 20 percent of their clients, international business travelers. Once the agents understood who their target market was, they were able to focus their priority responses, training and promotions toward providing better service to that top 20 percent. The result was increased customer retention in their target market with a proportional increase in sales due to their focus on the areas where the momentum toward their Vision was the highest. Focusing on your target market helps you replace the work that doesn't give you much momentum toward your Vision with work that does.

> Focusing on your target market helps you replace the work that doesn't give you much momentum toward your Vision with work that does.

One of our clients culled their bottom 20 percent of clients and became profitable immediately, freeing up some much-needed resources to service their priority clients. Another client was appalled to learn that the referrals they were receiving from a competitor were all very demanding, generated little revenue, and were as a result un-profitable accounts. These referrals were distracting the company from their target market.

The decision to maintain the 80 percent of your business that provides you with 20 percent of your momentum belongs to you, the business leader. At a minimum, it is critical for you to make yourself and others aware of who the top 20 percent of your customers are.

Focus on Your Target Market

Use your top Strategic Choices to focus your target market and priority product analysis. For example, if you have a catering company with a Vision of being known as the best caterer in the area, you could look at your list of customers and identify which of them are the most interested in purchasing the highest quality catering, and are prepared to pay for it. These clients will give this caterer the most momentum towards fulfilling their Vision. With the list of newly identified clients firmly in hand this company is prepared for the next level of analysis. To discover the characteristics common to those clients, which can then be used as search criteria to find more.

....

Your Strategic Choices formed your Vision and in the same way they focus your investigation of who your primary customers are, and what your primary products and services should be.

A dry cleaning business developed a strategy that includes specializing in imported rugs. They reviewed their receipts to identify who has been bringing in rugs to be cleaned. They discovered that most of the rugs were brought in by house cleaners for the homes where they cleaned. The dry cleaner then initiated a marketing program attractive to, and focusing on, house cleaners and the agencies that employed them.

Your Vision drives the identification of your target market. Your Strategic Choices formed your Vision and in the same way they focus your investigation of who your primary customers are and what your primary products and services should be. The first step in this analysis is to identify customers from your sales records who are attracted to your newly developed Vision. The second step is to identify meaningful characteristics common to those customers. Armed with a profile of your ideal customer you are ready to go find more of them!

Here are some hints to help you focus in on your target market and priority products or services:

Clarify if it is best for your company to start with customer type or product/service type. How do you organize your sales records today? Do you keep records based on the type of customer? For example, a CPA firm may track their client load by the size of the clients. Other businesses or industries will have a tendency to track sales by the type of product or service sold, such as a car dealer, who tracks how many cars, of which year and model, were sold.

How your specific industry or company traditionally tracks its sales impacts what you see when you look at your sales. Take some time to reconsider if it is more important for you to identify sales by what was purchased (product type) or by who purchased it (customer type). Depending on your database capabilities and sophistication, your company may have the information in both formats.

Obviously there is an interdependent relationship between who your top customers are and what your top products or services are. The decision whether to begin your analysis with product versus customer type should be driven by your Strategic Choices. If you are Expertise driven then you would want to look at which customers are most interested in purchasing that expertise. If you are Market Responsive driven, by definition your market is already named. In which case it is more meaningful to start by analyzing which products or services provide you with the most momentum toward your Vision.

If you own a small café you may have a system that tracks all of your sales by menu item (product type). This can be a helpful analysis when ordering stock. However, it may not help you analyze what percentages of your customers are returning local residents versus tourists. If the café's Vision includes a Strategic Choice "to cater to local residents," then the information that 60 percent of your sales are from coffee will not help you understand how to better reach those residents.

Use common sense in choosing what volume of past sales to analyze. It is difficult to provide a single all-inclusive answer to what volume of past sales records to include in this analysis. For each type of business or industry the answer can be quite different. If you have a restaurant, you may just use the meal receipts and go back one or two weeks. If you are a professional service firm with 50 clients a year, you will find it more valuable to go back two or three years to get a large enough sample to work with. Use your common sense when selecting the sample size.

It is important to identify a large enough sampling of past sales records to conduct a valid analysis. At a minimum you should

> There is an interdependent relationship between who your top customers are and what your top products or services are.

be looking at a sample of between 40 and 60 sales transactions. The idea is to have a large enough sample of sales to be able to find trends and market characteristics that are consistent among either your top customers or your top products/services.

Gain New Insights and as a Result Define a Market Niche

Use your Vision to find new ways to see past customers and thus gain insight into how you can better focus your marketing efforts.

The final reason why it is critical to participate in an investigation of your products or services and customers is to gain new insights into who your target market *really* is. This is accomplished by looking at your customers and products through the lens of your Vision. We challenge you to go further than you have ever gone before in analyzing your historical sales data.

To get the most insight from this Stage Two analysis you will need to leave behind the old categories you have always used when looking at your customers and products. Too often businesses only perform a profitability or gross sales analysis of their past sales. This is fine if profitability or market domination are your only differentiators. However, because of this business school or banker's orientation, many companies never identify the characteristics of the specific market niche that is most attracted to their company's specific competitive advantage. We advocate including the profit margin in every analysis but also recommend you consider that profit is not the only differentiator that warrants exploration when analyzing your past and current sales data. Use your Vision to find new ways to see past customers and thus gain insight into how you can better focus your marketing efforts. Insights gained by other companies through a Stage Two analysis include:

- A real estate agent learns that it is not the geographic location or the average sales price that impacts his success. It is the fact that the client is at least a third-time homebuyer.

- A software developer realizes that identifying markets by *type* of industry has not been effective for them. Instead, they discover that identifying offices with the need to record multiple billing rates for each of their service providers is a more fertile field for prospecting.

◆ A poetry magazine realizes it is not the general public who buys and reads its magazines; it is poets looking for a place to be published.

◆ A house-cleaning agency discovers that their best customers are not yuppies, but instead are single and over 55 years of age.

◆ A transcription service recognizes that their most consistent customers are attorneys without any administrative support.

◆ A consulting firm recognizes that it is companies with more than one active owner that are more likely to need their services.

◆ A fence company discovers that the length of time the prospect has owned their property greatly impacts the likelihood of a successful sale.

Do all these insights represent rocket science? Probably not, in fact most target market discoveries make perfect sense *after* they are discovered. But for the business leader, this type of clarity can really make a difference. A software developer can quickly establish whether a specific service business needs their product. A consulting firm can ask one question at a networking event to establish if the contact they are talking to is a true prospect. The real estate agent can sort out his best prospects with an interactive Web page survey.

These companies are no longer looking at generic market categories such as industry, age group, size of company, or geographies. These default categories are often not helpful but are overly depended on because the information is readily available. These traditional categories are generally more convenient than they are valuable. The above companies have gone outside the traditional marketing "box" and made some unique discoveries about their target market that they can use to better qualify and

In fact most target market discoveries, make perfect sense after they are discovered.

target prospects. The result is significantly more focused and effective prospecting and marketing.

Think outside the categories traditionally offered by your industry. Once you have identified the sample, consisting of your top 20 percent of sales, the next step is to identify common characteristics among your target market or priority products. As we stated earlier, most businesses tend to track sales based on categories in common use by their industry. The categories you use to track sales are set up in your "chart of accounts." Where did your chart of accounts come from? Many companies adopt theirs from their experiences in other businesses, from the original founder of the business, or from some other source such as the "default" chart of accounts traditionally used in your industry. These categories may serve you well in doing what needs to be done to assess your business' bottom line. However, they may limit your ability to get new insights into your target market.

Many companies traditionally use one category for grouping their customers. For example, a law firm has traditionally grouped their customers by the lawyer who handles the account. This is logical and a common practice in the legal industry. Grouping customers by which lawyer provides the service is useful from an internal business management viewpoint. It helps the law firm calculate the percentage of time a single attorney is billed, plan staffing, and develop performance-related incentives. However, categorizing their customers in this way is not useful in giving the partners a clear picture of who those customers are or where to find more of them. If the attorneys were to reorganize their list of clients by the type of industry their clients are in, the size of the customer's business, or how they were introduced to their customers, a clearer more usable picture would emerge.

Your pre-determined categories may result in reluctance to use alternative groupings for looking at your customers or products and services, because that data may not be readily available or easily resorted. Once your internal tracking systems have been set up, it can be time consuming and challenging to change them. However, the potential for rewards is great. During the Stage Two analysis, develop new categories for a deeper understanding of your target market. If you look at your past sales the

> Your pre-determined categories may result in reluctance to usie alternative groupings for looking at your customers or products and services, because that data may not be readily available or easily resorted.

way you always have, you will only see what you have always seen. We challenge you to find new ways to look at your sales data and as a result, gain new insights into your true target market and priority products and services. This point is demonstrated by the Nine Life Rings Exercise (see Figure 8.2).

Likewise, successful analysis of your customers, products, or services requires going outside the invisible boxes you may have always used to group your customers, products, or services. For the business owner, each life-ring represents a product or customer category. For example, a hotel may track their sales data by the following categories:

FIGURE 8.2: Nine Life Rings

The challenge is to connect all nine life rings using only four straight connected lines without ever removing your writing instrument from the paper or going back on a line already drawn.

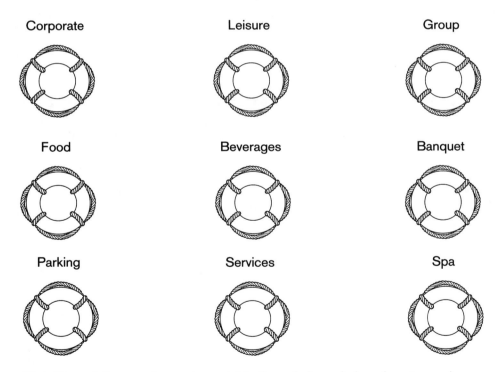

Hint: The solution requires going outside the safe boundaries of past experience.

The solution to Figure 8.2 is:

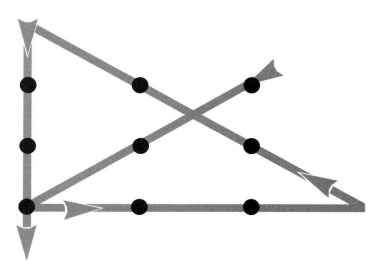

The lesson from this exercise is to look beyond predetermined boxes and categories to find new solutions. In creating a new focus for your business, it may be necessary to go beyond categories you have traditionally used to see your past sales data and future opportunities.

You may need to change the way you look at your past sales to gain new insight. Looking back at the law firm, they knew that their customers were divided equally among the three partners. They wanted to increase sales based on this information. Traditionally they would ask each partner to simply work harder. Instead they decided to consider working smarter. Working smarter means thinking strategically. After using alternative categories to identify the top 20 percent of their clients who are most attracted to the characteristics and capabilities leveraged by their business strategy, they discovered:

⊕ Professional contacts or referrals accounted for 74 percent of their sample.

⊕ Eight large accounts were 86 percent of the sample.

⊕ The high-tech industry had 78 percent of the sample.

....

In creating a new focus for your business, it may be necessary to go beyond categories you have traditionally used to see your past sales data and future opportunities from the perspective of your Vision.

◆ Requests to file intellectual property copyrights were 72 percent of the sample.

It is clear how critical this analysis will be if they plan to work smarter and focus on achieving their Vision. Using the above analysis, the partners understand whom to target (small high tech start-up firms referred to them by other professional service providers) and can work effectively to market their priority service (registering intellectual property rights and other projects that will lead to additional legal services in the future). At first it may seem like an overwhelming task to regroup and recalculate sales into new categories, but the pay-off in understanding your business is worth the investment.

When conducting your analysis, use the information available to you. Old sales records can be manipulated with some number crunching to provide new insight. You also have valuable experience and intuitive knowledge. In addition, you may want to design a system to test a hypothesis (or pre-judgment) you may have about your target market. For example, if you think that "women buy more cheese" you would ask your sales representatives to test that hypothesis by identifying the gender of your cheese buying customers. Remember you are looking for trends; reasonably accurate percentages can be very effective in proving or disproving a hypothesis. Check out Figure 8.3 for a sample of useful categories.

> *At first it may seem like an overwhelming task to regroup and recalculate sales into new categories, but the pay-off in understanding your business is worth the investment.*

Use the Results of the Analysis to Focus Your Business

The result of customer and product prioritization is a well-defined business focus. Once you have identified the characteristics of your target market and prioritized your products and services, you are ready to set your sales for success. Use your new insights to focus your marketing efforts and prioritize work. This new focus should be integrated with your sales goals, performance management, and accounting systems.

After creating new categories to analyze their customers, the legal firm is in a better position to understand what meaningful

FIGURE 8.3: Useful Catagories for Organizing Your Target Market and Highest Priority Products and Services

Type of customer industry:

- Customer business structure (sole proprietors, corporation, partnerships)
- Public or private companies
- Size of business by employees
- Size of business by gross sales
- Size of business by number of branches

Demographics of customer:

- Gender
- Age
- Educational level
- Income level
- Family size
- Marital status

Approaches for finding customer:

- Location of customers
- Times in which customers buy services
- Times in which customers use services
- Needs of customers
- Levels of quality required by customer
- Type of contract with customers
- Speed of delivery required
- Size of average sale
- Profitability of customer
- Number of annual sales per customer

Types of products or services:

- By materials used in production
- By size
- By skills required to provide service
- By designer
- By vendor

FIGURE 8.3: Useful Catagories for Organizing Your Target Market and Highest Priority Products and Services, continued

Ways in which products or services are delivered:

- Ways of selling products or services
- Types of packaging
- Length of services required
- Quality requirements and consistency
- Number of purchases per period
- Criteria for selection of vendors
- Types of products purchased
- Type of contract used
- Number of different types of products purchased

> Too often companies do not evaluate the assumptions they have about who their target market really is, and as a result they make poor business decisions.

characteristics are common amongst their priority customers. After a rigorous analysis, the partners can now develop strategic marketing plans, and refine their accounting and incentive systems instead of just asking each attorney to work harder. They realize that their old first-come, first-served mentality was not leveraging their business strategy, accelerating them toward their Vision, nor working to keep their priority clients satisfied. Too often companies do not evaluate the assumptions they have about who their target market really is, and as a result they make poor business decisions.

What Are Your Sales Objectives for the Next Financial Year

Set sales objectives consistent with what you learned from the analysis. The law firm would be well advised to set specific sales objectives (in support of their sales goal) for getting more high tech clients, increase the volume of their referral business, and develop their intellectual property practice.

We all have sales and profit objectives. Traditionally these objectives are developed by looking at historical performances, which are then projected forward. This is sometimes like trying to steer your car by looking through the rearview mirror. Focusing on a target market that supports your Vision requires setting sales objectives consistent with your Stage Two findings. If the attorneys continue to calculate their sales projections based on a percentage of billable hours per person, then that old system would prevent them from focusing on the type of customers they identified as being their target market. Take the helm and redesign the way you track and project sales.

> Focusing on a target market that supports your Vision requires setting sales objectives consistent with your Stage Two findings.

In Chapter 10 we provide detailed guidelines for setting the objectives your company will pursue over the next 12 months in order to accomplish your goals. We have found that the best time to set sales objectives is immediately following the analysis of your top priority customers and products. This makes setting them in alignment with your defined target market easier.

After finishing their analysis, the law firm rightly concluded they would be farther ahead by tracking the volume of new business they find in the high tech industry. Essentially they need to use a baseline that documents the volume of high tech business they have today (33 percent of their business is high tech), and then set objectives to increase that volume. The objective may be to have 55 percent of their net sales come from the high tech industry by the end of the fiscal year. Using your newly found understanding of your target market to set you sales objectives puts you dead-on course for your Vision.

If an architectural firm defines its Superiority as the design of water systems and they discover that their best projects are subcontracts with large national engineering firms, then it is time to stop right there and set a sales objective. One such objective could be: "By the end of the next financial year we will have relationships with ten large engineering firms, each giving us over 50K in subcontract work."

Setting a sales objective in alignment with your target market is an example of *working smarter*. Because of your analysis, you understand that business within your target market provides significantly more momentum toward your Vision. The above objective will serve this company far better than just setting a generic objective to "increase sales by 10 percent annually with projected sales of $750,000." This kind of traditional objective often results in a company simply *working harder.* Be a business leader: focus your team's energy on the target market and prioritized products or services.

Mission Statement

The results of your Stage Two decisions are summarized in the company Mission statement. A business Mission is a concise answer to the question: What does your company do? It clearly and specifically states:

- ◈ Who your highest priority customers are.
- ◈ What your primary products/services are.
- ◈ How you offer your products, that is unique (your number one Strategic Choice).

Your Mission statement is a summary of the Stage Two strategic decision-making.

Unlike the Vision statement, which is designed to be an *internal* document, the Mission is a company's most frequently used *external* statement. It is your primary communication tool. It should be incorporated in most company communications (verbal, written, and electronic), including almost all marketing materials. Your Mission statement is a summary of the Stage Two strategic decision-making. The Mission statement communicates the focus of your company.

Your Mission Statement Is a Tool for Attracting Your Target Market

A Mission statement is formulated to get your target market's attention. The point is to get your target market to focus on you by having them realize that you have focused your attention on them. Instead of "pushing" some kind of sales message, the Mission statement creates a vacuum that pulls your target market in.

It wasn't until the last century that mariners figured out a way to sail up-wind (any sales manager can tell you that generating sales is often an up-hill battle). Before the invention of the "marconi rig," square-rigged sailboats like the Nina, Pinta, and Santa Maria could basically sail only down wind (or at the very most 90 degrees to the wind). The new technology of rigging sails takes advantage of the way in which the wind, traveling across the front and back of a sail, creates a vacuum that actually pulls the boat forward into the wind. The Mission statement works in much the same way. By actually calling your target market's name you can create a vacuum that pulls your company toward your target market.

The owner of an engineering firm is on vacation in Europe and he is asked what he does. He answers with his Mission statement: "We work with multi-national utilities contractors to design infrastructures for the future. We offer engineering, site planning, and construction management services." The asking party, unbeknownst to him, was a member of his target market — a multi-national utility contractor. The next thing he knows he has an appointment with their office that results in his becoming connected to a huge opportunity. Now that is *pull marketing*. Before his company had a clear Mission he would have said he was an engineer and left it at that. What creates the *pull* is calling your specific target market's name in your Mission statement.

The following are some examples of phrases other companies use in their Mission statements to attract a specific target market:

- Sophisticated and experienced facility managers
- Cost-conscious consumers
- Discreet political campaign contributors
- Aggressive and dynamic developers
- Caring parents
- Locally owned and operated business founders
- Independent and successful professionals

....

Instead of "pushing" some kind of sales message, the Mission statement creates a vacuum that pulls your target market in.

⟡ Business leaders

As you read through this list, you knew whether a specific target market included you. For those that did, you may have noticed an inherent curiosity to learn what that company is and what they have to offer.

We work with business *owners* and CEOs, but we call them business *leaders* in our Mission statement because it is the business *owner* who is (or wants to be) a *leader* who is our target market.

....

Mission statements
should be clear,
concise, and usable.

Mission statements should be clear, concise, and usable. A good litmus test is can your Mission statement be used to answer the question: What does your company do?

The following are sample Mission statements:

⟡ A sailmaker's Mission may be to: "Prepare quality-conscious, serious, blue water cruisers with the finest off shore cruising sails, and hands-on sail handling, and sail maintenance training."

⟡ A technical institute's Mission may be to: "Prepare motivated students to be qualified computer programmers in today's business environment. We provide state-of-the-art training, practical experience, and job placement."

⟡ A community mortgage bank's Mission may be to: "Serve aggressive commercial real estate developers with consulting and financial services by finding and matching resources to meet our customers' needs."

⟡ A housing commission's Mission may be to: "Partner with community lenders to build financing programs for affordable housing through partnerships with developers, nonprofit organizations, and government agencies."

⟡ An architect's Mission may be to: "Collaborate with visionary leaders within our region to solve architectural challenges and provide innovative, sustainable, and enduring design solutions."

✦ Applied Business Solutions specializes in Strategic Planning tools. Our Mission is to provide business leaders with a comprehensive method for creating, strengthening, and maintaining a competitive advantage. Our proven Decision-Making process is available through seminars and retreats, customized consultations, books and workbooks, facilitator development, and public speaking presentations.

A Mission Statement is a Specific, Concise, and Consistent Message from Your Company to the World

A Mission statement is the number one communication tool that tells the world who you are in the business of serving and what you do. As a result it is wise to spend some time clarifying the wording, and then ensuring that everyone in your company uses the Mission to tell the world about your business. Take a walk through your company and offer a fresh $10 bill to any employee (or customer) who can recite your current Mission statement verbatim. Unfortunately this exercise probably won't cost you a dime.

If you have a business Mission but no one is using it there are generally three reasons.

> A Mission statement is the number one communication tool that tells the world who you are in the business of serving and what you do.

1. It does not really say what the company does.
2. It is too long and includes too much miscellaneous information.
3. Your company has not committed the resources to educate everyone in the company about the importance and purpose of using the Mission.

Your Mission describes the business that is required to achieve your Vision. The Mission statement is commonly used as a communication tool with current and potential employees, all vendors and customers, and in introducing the business to prospects and referral resources.

The Mission statement has many uses.

✦ Use it in all of your marketing materials.

♦ Print it on your business cards.

♦ Post it in the customer reception area.

♦ Post it in employee areas.

♦ Print it on incentive gifts or company momentos.

♦ Use it in your recorded answering service.

♦ Include it in your e-mail auto-signature and on the bottom of your fax forms.

♦ Use it when introducing yourself and in all company presentations.

♦ Have the receptionist use it when answering the phone.

♦ Include it in all your proposals and business letters.

The Mission Statement Communicates Business Priorities

Consider everyone who participates in the operation of your business as part of a team, your crew. The Mission statement tells your team what your highest priority products or services are and who your highest priority customers are. Without that knowledge, employees cannot possibly work at their highest potential, you cannot maximize their efforts, and valuable resources will be wasted. Confusion over which customers to serve first and how to serve them is detrimental to the achievement of your Vision and can easily be the result of not having a widely shared Mission statement. Every employee in the company should know the Mission and the Stage Two decisions it summarizes. Your Mission statement is exactly that, a mission. It is the purpose of the company. It is hard to imagine how your crew could contribute 100 percent of their potential to help achieve your company's Vision or Mission if they do not know or understand it.

We have found that when team members participate in the Mission writing exercise and understand the importance of the decisions that were made prior to developing the Mission statement, they are able to recreate the Mission without even having to memorize it.

> The Mission statement tells your team what your highest priority products or services are and who your highest priority customers are.

Over time you will want to revisit your Mission statement and the decisions that led up to it. Ask yourself: "How have our priorities changed since we wrote our Mission?" Our experience is that annual revisions may only include two or three word changes versus radical restatement of the Mission.

The Vision statement is a summary of the decisions made in Stage One strategic decision-making. The Mission statement is a summary of the decisions made in Stage Two strategic decision-making. Now that your Vision and Mission are established it is time to define the goals and objectives that turn your Vision into Action.

....

Over time you will
want to revisit your
Mission statement
and the decisions
that led up to it.

Goals

Before you can finish charting a course for your business you need to know not only the coordinates of your destination, but you must also have a clear understanding of your business' current position.

Your business is a vessel for achieving your dreams. Transforming those dreams into a viable and compelling Vision and Mission was the focus of Stages One and Two. Your Vision describes your business' destination in five to ten years. Your Mission pinpoints the exact coordinates of that destination (the intersection of your target market and your prioritized products or services). Are you prepared to set sail for your destination now? Not quite. Before you can finish charting a course for your business you need to know not only the coordinates of your destination, but you must also have a clear understanding of your business' current position.

When someone calls and asks for directions to your place of business, what is the most important piece of information that must be elicited from the caller before you can answer? "Where are you coming from?"

In Figure 9.1 your Vision defines Point B, but before you can chart a course to Point B you must assess where you are today, (Point A) relative to your Vision. With these two positions clear-

FIGURE 9.1: Plotting a Course From Where Your Business Is Today

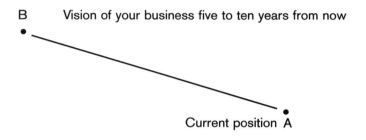

ly mapped out, the appropriate context has been created for setting goals and objectives, the operational components of strategic decision-making.

Goals are general areas of emphasis requiring a company's investment of time, energy, and money. Goals focus resource allocation and provide the framework within which management agrees on annual objectives. Annual objectives (covered in the next chapter) are the specific expectations that you use to hold your team accountable for achieving each goal. Goals are the result of Stage Three decision-making. Objectives are the result of Stage Four strategic decision-making.

The first step in setting goals is to begin with a survey to assess your company's current position. After reviewing the company's current position, you will be able to set a specific course in the form of realistic goals. In order to implement your strategy it is essential to set goals. Goals focus your company's efforts into manageable tasks. Without them your Vision remains merely a dream. Setting goals establishes accountability. It answers the question: "What do we need to operationalize in order to get us from Point A to Point B?"

> Goals focus resource allocation and provide the framework within which management agrees on annual objectives.

A Vision Without Action is Merely a Dream

Many people have dreams, but successful people transform their dreams into a Vision, then their Vision into Action. Now is the time to start putting your Vision into Action. This chapter provides you with tools to develop clearly-defined goals on which your company can focus its efforts over the next two to five years. Goals define operational expectations. The achievement of each goal brings you closer to the realization of your Vision.

Goals Focus Your Company's Efforts Into Manageable Areas

Often, a company that has a lofty Vision but no concrete goals feels like their Vision is not attainable, and will simply go back to business as usual.

Knowing that you want to build a reputation as the best engineering team specializing in environmental assessments is a worthy Vision. But to make that Vision attainable, you must set goals and realize them. Often, a company that has a lofty Vision but no concrete goals feels like their Vision is not attainable, and will simply go back to business as usual. Setting realistic, attainable goals is necessary to actualize the strategic decisions made in Stages One and Two. It is the achievement of goals that marks your progress towards success.

Goal Setting Is a Tool for Involving Others

The captain of a ship may be responsible for identifying the vessel's destination (Vision and Mission) but then it is time to get the rest of the crew involved. The captain needs a crew to help raise the sails and keep the vessel moving. Goal setting is an excellent time to expand involvement in your strategic decision-making. The more your crew understands about your goals, the more they are able to contribute to a successful passage.

Expand the number of people you are involving in your strategic decision-making. You may have been working independently, with a partner or an executive management team, on your strategic decisions. The number of people you've involved depends on the size of your company and your management style. However at this point, when you are deciding how to operationalize your strategy, consider including more of your team.

Including others in the goal-setting process is likely to bring a more honest assessment. Other people tend to ask questions like: "Why have you always done it that way?" You may choose to involve your employees and/or your customers in the goal-setting process. They are the best source of data for assessing your current position. You are also likely to find them invaluable in suggesting new solutions. If you do not have employees to include, consider involving your customers, vendors, or other trusted advisers.

Your primary customers are a great source of information because they will tell you:

- How you are performing in relationship to your stated Vision and Mission.

- What they like about your current products and services.

- What they don't like.

- What changes they may require of your products/services in the future.

An additional benefit to including your primary customers in this process is that it strengthens the partnership between you and your customers. Your customers will know that you are listening to, and watching out for, their needs. They will know that they can come to you with their ideas. The goodwill this creates is priceless.

Your key employees are a great source of information because they will tell you:

- How you are performing in relationship to your stated Vision and Mission.

- What inconsistencies they see in the way you do business.

- What threats they are aware of to your ongoing success.

- What will be required to operationalize your vision.

> Including others in the goal-setting process is likely to bring a more honest assessment.

> Your employees are an invaluable source of information. They are intimately involved in the day-to-day operations.

Your employees are an invaluable source of information. They are intimately involved in the day-to-day operations. It is a mistake not to elicit and use their feedback. They often know which systems are working, where the logjams are, and where the waste is. In addition to their input, involving your employees in Stages Three and Four is an excellent way to strengthen their understanding and commitment to the strategic direction of the business. It is our firm belief that your employees are one of the most valuable assets to your success. Their observations and insights should be included in the goal-setting process. Use Worksheet 8 to consider who you want to involve in the setting of goals.

WORKSHEET 8: Who Do You Intend to Involve in Your Goal Setting Process?

Which employees' input do you want to gather prior to setting your company's goals?

_____

_____

_____

Which customers' input do you want to gather prior to setting your company's goals?

_____

_____

_____

Which other trusted advisers would it be wise to include?

_____

_____

_____

Develop a Strategic Management Process

Your strategic plan is the foundation for what we call *strategic management*. In the beginning of this book we explained how a strategic plan creates the context for making day-to-day operational decisions consistently and with clarity. Strategic management means sticking to your plan. Plan what you do, then do what you planned!

....

Strategic management
means sticking to
your plan.

Experienced business leaders are probably thinking "Yeah, right. Easier said than done." There are challenges that must be overcome in order to succeed. But remember that it takes just as much, if not more, work to run a business that has no defined destination as it does to direct a business that is taking you to your preferred future. The major difference is that your job changes from being the business owner to being the business leader. Instead of being an expert on how to do a job, you become the expert in defining the right job to do. The real work of a business owner, principal, or senior executive is to set strategy and direct the business. One of our aims throughout this book has been to help you, the business leader, shift your focus.

Choosing the Right Goals

Choosing the right goals immediately overcomes the two biggest challenges to strategic management: Trying to achieve too many goals or the wrong goals.

Having too many goals will simply leave you and your crew feeling overwhelmed, uninspired, and unmotivated. The point of strategic decision-making is to focus your efforts, not add to them. All the activities that are essential to running your business should be addressed in the goal and objective setting processes. Instead of just adding goals, replace the ones that do not contribute directly to the achievement of your company's Vision. Choosing the wrong goals dilutes your resources and confuses your team. You'll know you've chosen the "right" goals if you can answer yes to: "Does this goal support the characteristics and capabilities we have chosen to set our business apart?"

It is traditional for a business to set sales and profit goals. However, sales and profit goals alone do not generally provide enough operational leadership for a company to be effectively managed towards a greater Vision. You may need to set goals to retain your current clients, develop new products, or attract and retain human resources. The shared Vision of the business with its associated goals will empower others to make the appropriate decisions.

We were working with a business that had recently merged into a larger company. The larger company told them that they could remain autonomous as long as they retained a 20 percent growth rate annually and 15 percent profit. In addition they tied the owner's final buyout amount to the company's next two years' growth and profit performance. Guess what happened? The owner stopped making quality customer service a priority, stopped investing in systems and staff training, and instead focused solely on the bottom line. They knew their only goals were based on profit and growth and they were going to be rewarded for their short-term thinking. There were no other clearly stated goals and objectives they were being held accountable for. This is an extreme example, and a true story, and the principles apply to every business.

Be sure to set goals in each of the operational areas that need to be invested in to ensure you achieve your Vision. For most companies those areas include a lot more than just sales and profit goals. Your company may also require that you set goals in one or more of the following areas:

- Customer relationship goals, including specific objectives directed at customer retention.

- Delivery, operations, or infrastructure goals, including specific objectives to make access to your products or services more available.

- Marketing goals to expand company name and recognition with your target market.

- Human Resource goals that include hiring, training, developing, and retaining good people.

> You may need to set goals to retain your current clients, develop new products, or attract and retain human resources.

◆ Product or service development goals, including specific objectives to either improve the quality or the breadth of your product line.

◆ Sales goals, including specific objectives to expand the percentage of the work you do with your target market or sales of your priority products or services.

◆ Profit goals, including specific objectives to increase firm equity and fiscal security.

Guidelines for Assessing Your Company's Current Position and Setting Goals

Accurately assessing your company's position relative to your business Vision is an important step in the successful identification of your business goals. Use a SWOT (Strengths, Weaknesses, Opportunities & Threats) survey to reveal which operational areas require an investment of company resources in order to achieve your Vision. Whether you choose to use a SWOT survey or some other method, we offer the following guidelines for eliciting useful responses and determining your company's position.

> It is difficult if not impossible to assess the strengths and weaknesses of a vessel if you don't appreciate what its intended uses are.

Communicate Your Vision and Mission

Because we are avid sailors our friends like to involve us in helping them choose the right boat when they are preparing to make a purchase. It is always fun to go kick some hulls and make an assessment, but before anything that we say can be meaningful, it is important for us to appreciate where they are planning to take the boat. Being lightweight and easy to trailer is a strength for a lake boat, but it becomes a weakness if the intention is to take it out onto the open ocean. It is difficult, if not impossible, to assess the strengths and weaknesses of a vessel if you don't know what its intended uses are. It is important to inform anyone you are asking to assess your business, where you intend to take it.

You will get much more useful feedback if you clearly communicate what you expect your company to look like in the future before you ask for input on what is required to get it there.

If you look at the average market survey or post-purchase survey (the surveys that are now available in many retail service outlets) you will notice that there isn't a place for the company to indicate its market niche, Vision, or Mission. As a result, the respondent provides feedback, but the feedback may not be particularly relevant or useful. Presenting the priorities set forth in your Vision and Mission to survey respondents results in their ability to give you much more valuable feedback.

An example of how you can increase the value of your feedback is a short evaluation card handed out with the receipt by a hairstylist employed at a large salon chain. One of the questions on the survey asks the recipient to rate the stylist. The options given on the survey are: poor, average, good, excellent. As the respondent, you have to make the evaluation, but the question arises: "As compared to what?" You may evaluate the stylist based on any number of Strategic Choices:

- Consistency of style from visit to visit.
- The speed of the stylist.
- The quality of the style.
- The innovation of the style.
- The personality of the stylist.

How helpful will this survey be if 75 percent of the respondents say good, 20 percent say average, and the other 5 percent excellent? What will management have really learned? Your feedback would be much more valuable to the salon if they had told you their Vision and asked for contradictions between it and your perception of the stylist. For example, the response card could clearly indicate the salon's strategy is to be "known for the most creative stylists in town," or "committed to providing you with

Presenting the priorities set forth in your Vision and Mission to survey respondents results in their ability to give you much more valuable feedback.

a consistent hair style every visit," or "committed to the fastest style in the West." Only when you know the strategy are you able to provide helpful feedback, using specific criteria to evaluate the stylist.

Ask for the contradictions between your Vision and your current operations. Once people know your Vision, you can ask for specific feedback and find the contradictions between your Vision and the way you are actually operating. With this information in hand you are prepared to set goals that close the gap between where you are today and where you want to be tomorrow.

If your Vision includes being Distribution driven, yet your customers indicate that they do not have good access to your products and services, this feedback represents an opportunity for improvement. The results suggest you should set a goal to enhance your distribution network.

The same would be true if your Vision included being Human Resource driven and yet your employees reported your compensation package is one of your weaknesses. Again, the feedback points to an area for setting a goal. The goals, based on your internal and external customer feedback, will provide the focus that propels your company forward.

When Developing a Survey, Ask a Few Simple Questions

Use a simple SWOT survey to assess your current position. A SWOT survey can be easily designed to gather data about your business' current strengths, weaknesses, opportunities, and threats as it relates to your Vision and Mission. The purpose of the survey is to identify areas that require your attention, energy, and resources. Once you have identified which areas to focus on, you can set specific goals. Remember: Always use a SWOT from the perspective of the voyage you are planning to undertake.

> Once people know your Vision, you can ask for specific feedback and find the contradictions between your Vision and the way you are actually operating.

Before leaving on a significant passage, the captain and crew work together to survey the vessel. Keeping in mind what kind of passage they are about to undertake, they inspect the vessel, making note of:

- Strengths and how to build on them.
- Weaknesses and how to fix them.
- Opportunities and how to take advantage of them.
- Threats and how to avoid or address them.

The SWOT survey helps you define where your company is today and identify critical areas that require change. We encourage you to go out and gather information in the best ways possible given your time, schedule, and budget. Plan to survey your employees and customers, but don't get stuck in the logistics of the survey process. Surveying is a science and an art. There are many professional firms that can help you write a survey and analyze the results. These firms are helpful, but they are not essential.

The first time you gather data, you will have more information than you have ever had in the past, even if the survey is not perfect. Each year, as you go through your strategic planning cycle, the process, the quality, and the validity of information you collect will improve. For your first round, even if only ten people participate in a very simple SWOT process, you will be significantly further ahead in your goal-setting process. The results of your SWOT survey comprise the foundation of your goal-setting process.

Ask Open-Ended Questions to Elicit More Complete Responses

Use open-ended questions to gather information. Open-ended questions provide you with more information and maybe some surprises. Close-ended questions can only be used to confirm or disprove what you already expect to hear. Open-ended questions start with W's or H's (how, who, when, what, where, why); close-ended questions start with verbs like: are we, do

> The SWOT survey helps you define where your company is today and identify critical areas that require change.

we, can we, should we, and so on. Close-ended questions are traditionally preferred on surveys because the results are easier to summarize, analyze, and report. However, the goal of your survey is not easy reporting, it is to gather information. Open-ended questions require more than a check mark or one- or two-word answers. The difference in functionality between open and close-ended questions is demonstrated by this example with the XYZ Corporation.

Vision

XYZ Inc. is committed to five-day service for your ordered parts.

"Should we reduce the time it takes us to ship an order?" (close-ended)

"What are your reactions to our order shipping time?" (open-ende*d)*

The close-ended question contains an assumption — that a shorter period for delivery is desirable. This may or may not be the case. Perhaps the respondent is more interested in receiving accurately filled orders than a quicker response time. The close-ended question limits the response you will receive. You will elicit much more valuable information by using open-ended questions that do not contain assumptions.

The straightforward approach is the best. Start with: a statement of your Mission, a statement of the strategic priorities that are the components of your Vision, and/or your marketing slogan. Then you can ask some straightforward questions like: "Based on our Mission …

… what are our strengths?"

… what are our weaknesses?"

… what are our opportunities?"

… what threats to our business' success should we be watching out for?"

> The goal of your survey is not easy reporting, it is to gather information.

Two-Way Communication

Two-way communication with your employees and customers ensures you have the opportunity to ask additional questions and clarify their input. Whether it is possible to have two-way communication depends on the number of people you choose to involve and the logistics of surveying them. Two-way communication will increase the value of the information you receive during the SWOT survey process. There are several ways to gather data using two-way communication, including interviews, focus groups, and phone surveys.

Choose the best survey technique for your company based on your resources. Some companies get tied up in the size of the sample, validity of the measurement tool, or statistical reporting of the results. These issues are important; however, the most important thing is to: *Just Do It*. Seventy-three percent of the companies we have surveyed do not gather data as part of their goal-setting process. Even asking ten people four questions can put your company leaps and bounds ahead of the competition.

Remember strategic management is an ongoing process. Plan to gather employee and customer data frequently (annually) to keep your plan and your company's goals up-to-date with your internal and external customer expectations.

Revise Your Survey Now for Next Year

A survey has never been developed that answers all your questions. Even when you use a pilot survey (sending the survey out to a limited group in advance) and then revise the survey based on what you learned from the pilot, there are always additional questions you will want to ask in the next round of customer surveys. The best time to revise the survey is when you are analyzing and summarizing the results of the last survey. It is during the analyzing and summarizing process that the information you wish you had collected is freshest in your mind.

> Whether it is possible to have two-way communication depends on the number of people you choose to involve and the logistics of surveying them.

Summarize Your Survey Feedback

Use the results of your survey to set goals. The wealth of information you receive from your survey is helpful in identifying the most important areas for your company to focus on in order to achieve your Vision. Remember the survey is designed to gather data on the discrepancies between your stated Vision and Mission and how you currently do business. You then use the data from the survey to identify goals.

Categorize the feedback into general themes. Use your survey data to look for major points that come up from several sources. Look for areas identified in your survey as critical, requiring attention and resources in order to achieve your Vision. The SWOT survey process encourages companies to set goals that will build on current strengths, correct weaknesses, take advantage of opportunities, and actively address threats.

> The wealth of
> information you
> receive from your survey
> is helpful in identifying
> the most important
> areas for your company
> to focus on in order to
> achieve your Vision.

Use the Survey Results to Set Company Goals

Identifying and working towards specific goals coordinates and organizes the efforts of your company. Create goals that accent or enhance your company's movement toward your Vision. The survey will inform you of areas requiring company goals in addition to your profit and gross sales goals. Use the results of the survey to set your two to five-year goals.

Set goals that:

- Are consistent with your Mission.
- You can realistically achieve.
- Correct weaknesses and take advantage of opportunities.
- Build on strengths and proactively address threats.

Define five to seven areas in which you want to set goals. Any more than seven company goals will divide and dilute your company's resources too much. Goals are set with the intention of being achieved over the next two to five years. This is a good time-frame for setting goals because it generally takes a company at least two to five years to fully realize major changes in their operations. However, your goals may require modifying before the end of the five-year period. We recommend you revisit your SWOT process and goals annually.

Goals are general areas in which the company chooses to invest its resources over the next five to ten years. Some examples of goal areas include:

- Strengthen marketing and company visibility.
- Develop a system to manage and gain access to historical data.
- Strengthen product procedures and delivery systems.
- Establish strategic alliances and sub-consulting relationships.
- Increase sales to target market.
- Provide adequate staff training and incentives to reduce staff burnout and increase retention.
- Make wise business decisions that result in a profit.

Once you have identified a comprehensive list of potential goal areas, select the top five to seven goals that are the highest priority for achieving your Vision. Include the two traditional business areas in your five to seven goals: gross revenues/sales and profits. These goals are important. The SWOT process will help you expand your business management by providing focus on operational requirements to achieve your Vision as well as the profitability of the business.

Provide feedback to the people who participated in the assessment. Involving others in setting goals is an important step toward eliciting their assistance in achieving your goals. Use two-way communication to demonstrate you honor their input. Report to everyone what you learned on your survey and how you used that information to set your goals.

> Goals are general areas in which the company chooses to invest its resources over the next five to ten years.

In the next chapter be prepared to take the helm by defining the specific, measurable objectives that actualize your goals and turn your Vision into Action.

CHAPTER 10

Objectives

Commit to following through with the goals and objectives that are required to turn your Vision into Action. Set realistic and attainable goals and objectives. In Chapter 9 the guidelines for identifying five to seven goals for your company were provided. The purpose of those goals is to direct your company's energy and resources over the next two to five years. Goals, in turn, are then supported by more specific expectations called objectives. Objectives state the incremental actions you commit to take, and the outcomes you expect to achieve in the next 12 months to realize each of your goals. We speak of well thought out objectives as being SMART. SMART is an acronym that stands for Specific, Measurable, Agreed upon, Results-Oriented, with a Tracking system. In general, each goal has an average of five supporting objectives. Figure 10.1 describes the relationship between goals and objectives.

Objectives state the incremental actions you commit to take, and the outcomes you expect to achieve in the next 12 months to realize each of your goals.

Setting objectives is an essential step in the implementation of your strategic decisions. It is akin to raising and setting the sails on a boat. Once they are in place, the momentum starts

FIGURE 10.1: Relationship Between Goals and Objectives

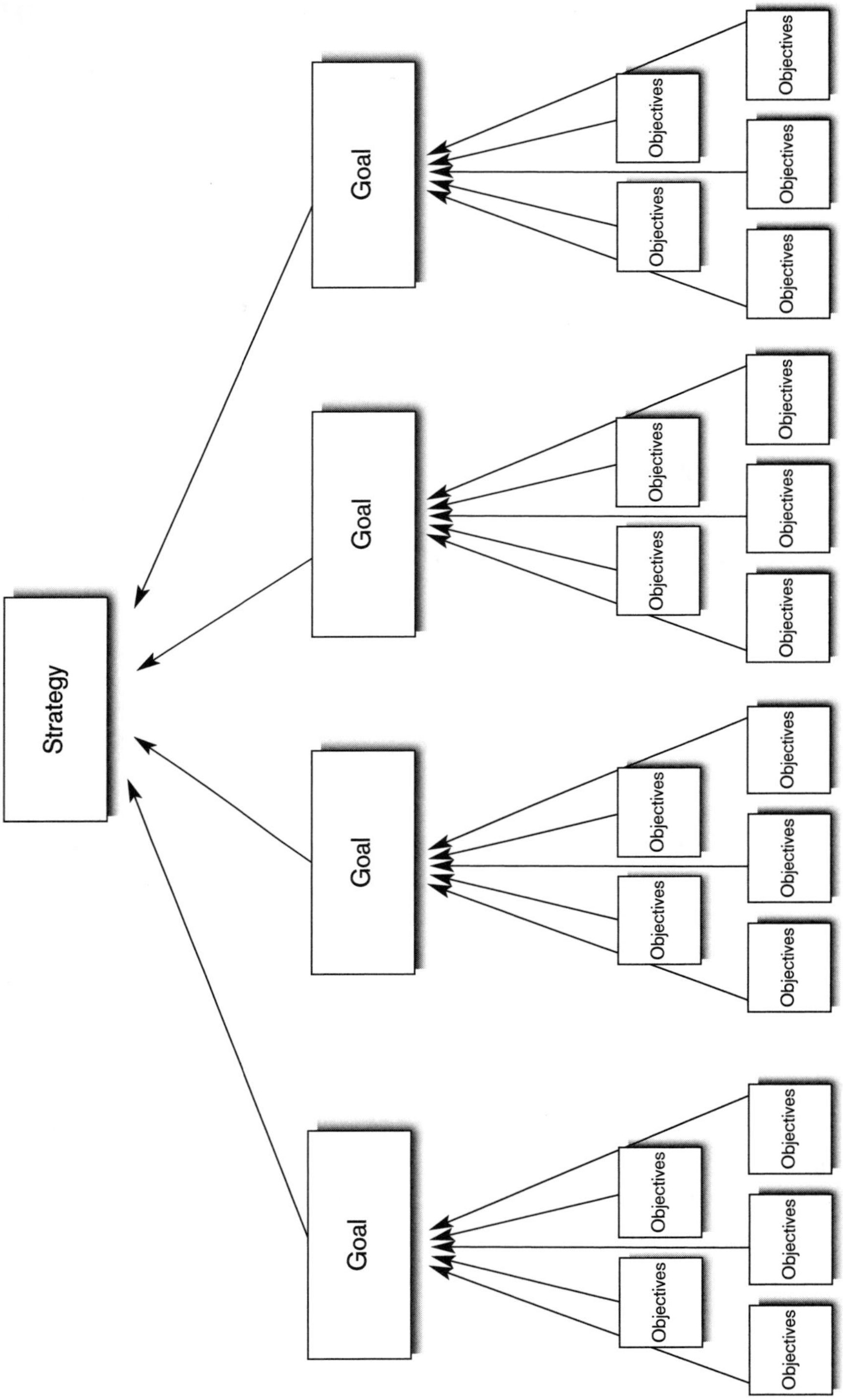

Objectives are the results you want to achieve.

building. In this chapter we present the guidelines for setting result-oriented, SMART objectives to support your company goals.

Before departing on a passage, the savvy skipper draws the intended course on a chart. Then the objectives or milestones that can be realistically achieved are marked off as the vessel completes its passage. During the passage the speed and distance traveled are tracked and compared continuously with the course. In this way the captain is always aware of the current position and knows when it is necessary to adjust the course. Each objective achieved is one step closer to the final destination of the Vision. How quickly you achieve your Vision depends largely on how much you are willing to invest in achieving each particular goal.

Why Set Annual Objectives?

Setting annual objectives is essential because they clarify realistic performance expectations and signal your commitment to turning your Vision into Action.

Clarify Realistic Performance Expectations

Objectives clarify the performance expectations you have of yourself, your company, and your team.

Objectives state the results you expect to achieve over the next 12 months in specific and measurable terms. Writing SMART objectives is an integral step in operationalizing your strategic decisions and setting clear expectations that you and your crew are accountable for achieving. Setting objectives is a communication tool and management responsibility. Objectives clarify the performance expectations you have of yourself, your company, and your team.

Goals are general areas that direct your company resources. For example, in the last chapter a company identified "strengthen marketing and company visibility" as a critical goal area. This is a good example of a goal; however, not until objectives are developed to achieve it, will it be clear *who* has to do *what* by *when* to achieve that goal. SMART objectives for the above goal may include: sending out press releases monthly or ensuring that 50 percent of our prospects are familiar with your name before your salesperson contacts them.

Writing SMART objectives is the first step in successful delegation. Without clearly defined expectations in the form of objectives, it is difficult for business leaders and managers to successfully delegate responsibility to others. You, as a business leader, need to take the time to set objectives. It will be difficult for anyone on your team (including yourself) to know what is expected, how much it will cost, what the return on the investment might be, or when you have succeeded in making incremental progress toward your goals. SMART objectives meet the following criteria:

Specific: Pinpoint the exact performance levels expected.

Measurable: Develop a system for calibrating movement toward the goal; identify criteria for the successful completion of the objective.

Agreed upon: Discuss with and ask for commitments from the people who will help you achieve the objective.

Results-oriented: Clearly define the results you expect.

Trackable: Develop a management system for tracking performance. Define how you will measure success.

Commit to Turning Your Vision Into Action

Complete your strategic decision-making process by defining SMART objectives and committing the resources to turn your Vision into Action. Each of your objectives will cost resources (time, attention, or money) to implement. Once you have identified preliminary SMART objectives, you can begin the process of budgeting to ensure the resources are available to support their implementation. The allocation of resources is the final decision made in the four stage decision-making process. Objectives signal your commitment and control the speed at which your company changes course. Creating a budget is greatly simplified by utilizing SMART objectives.

Without clearly defined expectations in the form of objectives, it is difficult for business leaders and managers to successfully delegate responsibility to others.

For example, you have a goal to enhance your company's exposure to your target market. Once you define your objective, to place quarterly ads in four selected trade journals, the cost of implementing that objective can be researched and built into your budgeting process. SMART objectives are critical if you are really going to allocate the resources necessary to achieve your goals.

The amount of resources you invest will impact how quickly you reach your Vision. Your business strategy determines the direction in which your business is heading, and your Strategic Choices are the engines that power it forward. Those engines require fuel in the form of resources: time, energy, and money. How many resources you are able to allocate to each engine determines how fast your business will move toward its destination. The final reality checkpoint in the strategic decision-making process is the allocation of resources. If one of your top four Strategic Choices is driven by technology and your budget simply won't allow for your business to stay on the "bleeding edge" for long, then you either have to rethink your strategy, create an objective to raise capital, or be prepared for a slower passage. If you have set a goal or objective that is beyond your company's resources then you will need to slow down and set a more realistic objective.

....

Your business strategy determines the direction in which your business is heading, and your Strategic Choices are the engines that power it forward.

Guidelines for Writing SMART Result-Oriented Objectives

Identify the Annual Objectives Required to Achieve Your Goals

You have the tools to define the five to seven goal areas required to turn your Vision into Action. Now it is time to agree with your team on *how* you will make progress toward achieving those goals. The process of identifying SMART objectives is also ideal for expanding involvement from within your company. Involve everyone whom you will expect to hold responsible for achieving those objectives. Involving others increases commitment and leadership. For each goal area you have defined, you will develop two to five SMART objectives. The outcome will be to identify between 10 and 35 objectives for the next year.

SMART objectives define your company's work over the next year. They should include the initiatives you are already investing in that contribute to achieving your goals (and ultimately your Vision), as well as the new objectives you and your team have identified. For each goal area you will find it helpful to consider:

- What are we currently doing which is contributing to this goal?
- What should we stop doing?
- What should we continue doing?
- What should we start doing?

Your business objectives define your operational expectations and should be replacing or simply reinforcing the operational expectations presently in place. Whatever operational expectations you had in place prior to creating your strategic plan should either be integrated as one of the 10 to 35 objectives, or removed. Some of those expectations may have been written down, and so can easily be reviewed to see how they fit in. Then can be the appropriate action taken. Other operational expectations tend to just float around. It is a good idea to sit down with your management team and record those expectations so they can be included or excluded as appropriate.

For example, a small medical clinic organized process improvement teams several years ago with the objective of responding to patient feedback and staff suggestions. They wish to continue pursuing this objective and so it is simply placed under their new goal: "To improve and create a caring and healing environment." Making sure this objective gets positioned under a goal integrates it into the resource planning process and reinforces it as an important ongoing commitment of the clinic. In addition, it legitimizes the investment as a tool for attaining the company Vision.

Your business objectives define your operational expectations and should be replacing or simply reinforcing the operational expectations presently in place.

On the other hand, the clinic has always hosted a small fund-raising activity for their community hospital. As a result of choosing goals that were in better alignment with their new Vision, they realized that the "real goal" was to: "Provide leadership in the community." They saw that their small fund-raising efforts were very time consuming and did not generate significant funds nor provide many leadership opportunities. So they chose to reallocate the time they had previously invested in coordinating this event into an objective that better matched their clarified goal. The new objective became "to have all six of their key staff actively participating as leaders on the boards of major nonprofit organizations."

Your strategic plan creates the context for making these types of operational decisions now, and on an ongoing day-to-day basis. It is important not to pile objectives on top of older objectives that no longer help the company achieve its goals. This type of "adding on" will simply overwhelm your staff. Instead, assess your current objectives and continue those that really help you achieve your goals. Then you can re-allocate resources to the new objectives best suited for achieving your goals.

It is also better to identify and achieve 20 well thought out objectives than to set 35 objectives that overwhelm your company with expectations and lose the focus on the plan. It is your job, as the leader, to ensure that your company does not develop too many objectives. The strategic question of "which" remains the responsibility of the leader. In this case it is: "Which objectives are most critical for us to make progress toward our goals?" and "Which objectives are the most critical for us to invest our limited time, resources, and focus in achieving our goals?"

There is a great difference between this process and the one developed in the late 1970s, called management by objectives (MBO). In the MBO process the purpose was to define objectives for individuals on all levels in the organization; however, in our process the purpose is to identify the "right" objectives for the company as a whole, allowing for tighter focus on the strategic plan and a solid commitment to implementation.

> Your strategic plan creates the context for making these types of operational decisions now, and on an ongoing day-to-day basis.

Develop SMART objectives by reviewing your goals. For example, if you have decided on a goal "to expand employee ownership," then the next step is to decide what your expectations are in that area for the next year. In other words, what are you or others in the company going to do during the next 12 months to expand employee ownership? In addition, you want to agree on who will be responsible and what budget is available to be invested.

There are many ways to expand employee ownership, just as there are many ways to achieve each of your business goals. Start the process by looking at each of your goals. Brainstorm as many ways as possible to achieve each of them. The guidelines for brainstorming include:

....

Brainstorming is a tool for seeing new ways to achieve your goals.

◆ Letting ideas build on one another.

◆ Accepting all ideas; no idea is too silly to put on the list.

◆ Resisting the temptation to evaluate ideas as they come forward.

◆ Letting yourself and others think of as many ideas as possible.

◆ Adding additional ideas. Once you have run out of ideas, think of half again as many ideas to add to the list.

◆ Brainstorming until you have at least 25 ideas for each goal area.

Brainstorming is a tool for seeing new ways to achieve your goals. Make this a process of discovery, not a process of recording what you always thought you (or your staff) should be doing. Take the time to brainstorm creative ideas with others. Our experience has taught us that the first ideas identified are generally more expensive. As you continue to brainstorm, you will discover other objectives to achieve your goals. These objectives tend to be less expensive and more creative than the first ideas that surfaced. After you have finished brainstorming, you can go back and evaluate all the ideas that came up, and select the best ones. Ultimately you are looking for two to five great ideas to take forward into the next step in the process.

From a logistics standpoint, it is helpful to number the goals and then letter the objectives. As a result, you will have goal #1 with objectives A, B, and C, etc. Each objective under a goal heading is written 1A, 1B, or 2A, 2B, and so on.

Write Each Objective in Specific and Measurable Language

Transform your objective ideas by redefining them into SMART objectives.

The process of defining SMART objectives involves clarifying what you actually expect your company to achieve in the 12 months. Transform your objective ideas by redefining them into SMART objectives. SMART objectives should be achievable during the next fiscal year and will look like the following examples:

Goal	SMART Objectives
1. Increase sales of XYZ product	1A. Develop a market plan by Jan. 15 to increase sales of XYZ by 35 percent.
	1B. Increase our win ration on proposals to 85 percent.
2. Increase partners' profits	2A. Increase annual profits by 15 percent for the next fiscal year to $650,000.
3. Enhance professional image	3. Move into an office in downtown in community Mercer Island by June 1, 2001.

Notice how goals are general in scope, and how specific the objectives are? You know these are SMART objectives because you can go back and apply the SMART criteria. For example, look at objective 1A: Develop a marketing plan by January 15 to increase sales of XYZ by 35 percent.

S = This particular company has identified a *specific* performance level: a marketing plan by January 15.

M = It is *measurable,* because it has a defined product and a date. On January 15, the company will know if the objective has been achieved.

A = We will have to assume the objective was discussed and *agreed upon* with those responsible for achieving the objective.

R = The result (35 percent increase in sales) is clearly stated.

T = Finally, the *tracking system.* In this case the tracking system is simply follow-up to ensure that the marketing plan was indeed completed on schedule.

Objectives Have Measurement Systems

Defining appropriate measurements is a part of identifying SMART objectives and establishing your company's performance expectations over the next year. Identifying appropriate measurement systems can be challenging. Be sure your measures are consistent with, and reinforcing, your company Vision and selected differentiators.

Use two different methods to help you identify potential measurement systems during your objective writing process.

1. Make the measurements in your objectives consistent with your differentiators.

2. Look at what you are currently measuring.

Make the measurements in your objectives consistent with your differentiators. When writing SMART objectives, first review your differentiators for measurement criteria. Each of the differentiators has inherent measurement assumptions. Look at your differentiators and see what insight may be gained into the appropriate measurement systems you will want to incorporate when writing your SMART objectives.

....

Be sure your measures are consistent with, and reinforcing your company Vision and differentiators.

Market Response companies may:

- Measure, control, improve, and increase customer retention and customer return ratios.

- Measure customers' expectations and see an increase in satisfaction over time.

Product/Service Superiority companies may:

- Measure, control, improve, and increase the quality of the product.

- Track the number of product returns or repairs required or customers' perception of the product quality in comparison to similar products on the market.

Production Efficient companies may:

- Measure, control, improve, and reduce the cost of production, run times, volume of waste, and time required to produce a specific product or service.

Natural or Human Resource companies may:

- Measure, control, improve, and track the access to, and cost of, natural resources.

- Measure turnover, training time, and employee satisfaction rates.

Market Dominance companies may:

- Measure, control, improve, and increase the volume of sales, number of locations, and of course, market-share.

Short-Term Profit companies may:

- Measure, control, improve, and increase return on capital investments, cash flow, and short and long-term stockholder equity.

Look at your differentiators and see what insight may be gained about the appropriate measurement systems you will want to incorporate when writing your SMART objectives.

Method of Sales companies may:

◆ Measure, control, improve, and increase sales force, volumes of sales per outlet, the number of products represented, and the cost of sale.

Method of Distribution companies may:

◆ Measure, control, improve, and increase distribution efficiency, reduce cost of distributions, increase the introduction of new products and services, and reduce the time required for the customer to receive the product or service.

Technology companies may:

◆ Measure consistent volume of new products/services and application of leading edge technology, number of copyrights and patents, cost of research and development, and speed getting the product to market.

Look at what you are currently measuring. Look at how you are measuring progress toward your goals today because you may be able to incorporate these measures when writing your SMART objectives. Some businesses have baseline data they can use to identify measurable objectives, other companies need to start from scratch by identifying important measures and then developing the systems to track, record, and report on those measures.

Be sure your current measures are consistent with your differentiators. If quality is your differentiator, try to avoid using volume as the key measure in your objectives. For each goal area, identify the current level of performance. Once you have reflected on the best way to measure your progress toward each objective, you are prepared to define the most appropriate measurement systems and then develop a SMART objective.

Be sure your current
measures are consistent
with your differentiators.

Result-Oriented Objectives

Ideally you want to define "result-oriented" objectives. Result-oriented objectives clearly state the results you want to achieve over the following 12 months. A common mistake that many businesses make is to set too many *process*-oriented objectives instead of *result*-oriented objectives. For example, many of us have personal goals to "get in better physical condition in the New Year." Setting a *process*-oriented objective is like making a New Years' resolution to "go on a diet" or "join a health club." Going on a diet and joining a health club are processes; however, committing to a *process* does not mean you will get a *result*. Simply joining the health club does not guarantee you will go, or get in better physical condition.

Define the result: The result you want may be to lose ten pounds. Stating the result you want to achieve invites creativity and commitment to that outcome. For example, if you can lose ten pounds without going on the diet, wouldn't you be just as satisfied?

> Stating the result you want to achieve invites creativity and commitment to that outcome.

The true litmus test between a process-oriented objective and a result-oriented objective when applied to the business environment is the return on investment. The process-oriented objective costs money to implement but it is difficult to define the specific return on investment from achieving it. For example:

Process-oriented objective. Improve our sales management process through broker accountability and company incentives.

SMART, result-oriented objective. Increase each broker's book of business by 15 percent through the use of sales management, broker accountability, and company incentives.

Process-oriented objective. Implement bonus programs to increase an internal and external referral program.

SMART, result-oriented objective. Receive 25 percent of our new business through referrals by implementing bonus programs for internal and external referral resources.

Clarify the results you expect to achieve in your business objectives. Setting goals with objectives that are *result*-oriented provides leeway in how the objective is to be achieved, and invites others to take responsibility in accomplishing those objectives.

Clearly stating the result you expect empowers your team to take more responsibility in finding the process best suited to getting that result. The ideal role of the management team then becomes supporting people in achieving objectives and problem solving when an objective is not being met. This is different than having the management team agreeing on how to achieve a specific objective. Our experience is that moving from a process-oriented leadership style to a result-oriented leadership style is part of the natural evolution of a management team as they move from an entrepreneurship to a professionally managed business.

Know the results you want to achieve before you allocate the resources. The importance of knowing and recording the results you want to achieve is that you are less likely to invest in *processes* that do not guarantee the results you are looking for. It is far less effective to set *process* objectives such as "provide management training" or "develop a marketing plan" when what you really want is *results* like, "reduce employee turnover" and "increase sales in a specific market." Define in advance the results you expect to gain from making your investments in SMART objectives.

> The ideal role of the management team then becomes supporting people in achieving objectives and problem solving when an objective is not being met.

Estimate the Resources Required and ROI for Each Objective

Setting objectives is a critical management tool and the foundation for delegating tasks. Before you commit to achieving the objectives you have written, review the soundness of your financial decisions. Estimate resources required and the return-on-investment (ROI) for each of your objectives. Anticipate the overall financial results of implementing all of your objectives. Finally, clarify in advance if your objectives are realistic.

Too often, in the glow of a newly developed Vision, companies attempt to do too much in the first year. Most of your objectives will cost you valuable time, money, and energy to put into action. Ask yourself, "Is it realistic to invest our resources in the next year to achieve this objective?" Estimating the required resources and the ROI for each objective will keep you from over-committing your staff and resources.

Once you've estimated the resources required and the ROI for each objective, you may choose to postpone some objectives. Other choices may include agreeing to operate at a financial loss this year so that your company can be better positioned to perform next year, or planning to increase your gross revenues to support the achievement of the objectives. In any case, it's best for your company leadership to understand and agree upon one of the above conclusions before committing to implement all of the objectives.

> Estimating the required resources and the ROI for each objective will keep you from over-committing your staff and resources.

Develop the Project Management Plan

Developing a realistic budget for each of your SMART objectives will require doing a little project management. Delegate an individual to research the costs of implementing each of the objectives. Be sure to include both the "soft costs" associated with people time and the "hard costs," like any capital investment that will need to be made. In some cases, you cannot know the exact cost of implementing an objective or the potential ROI, but don't let your lack of surety be the reason for not estimating the financial results of implementing your objectives. Be a smart business leader. Require a preliminary survey of the decisions made, an estimate of the direct financial gain, and an estimate of the costs for implementing each objective.

Make a Decision about How Much You Can Afford to Invest in the Next Year

Once you have estimated the financial gains and projected costs of each objective, you can calculate the impact on your budget. Take the final step to ensure your objectives are realistic. Make decisions on *which* objectives you can commit to implement. Ask yourself: "Is my company willing to commit the resources required to achieve these objectives?"

The decision to implement your objectives is partially based on your estimate of the financial gain you anticipate receiving by achieving each objective. Take a look at the SMART objectives from the earlier example:

> 1A: Develop a market plan by January 15 to increase sales of XYZ by 35 percent.
>
> This is a process objective and there is no direct expectation of increased sales for the year, only the expectation of having a marketing plan with the intent to increase sales during a later business period.
>
> Estimated gain: $0

> 1B. Increase the win ration on proposals to 85 percent.
>
> Estimated gain: $150,000.

> 2A: Increase annual profits by 15 percent for the next fiscal year to $650,000.
>
> Estimated gain: $97,500

> 3A: Move into an office in downtown Mercer Island by June.
>
> Estimated gain: $0

The second half of the formula is to estimate the costs of implementing the objective. Take a look and see how it is done with the objectives from above:

> 1A: Develop a market plan by January 15 to increase sales of XYZ by 35 percent.
>
> You can estimate what it will cost you to develop a marketing plan. Some companies have internal staff to support this process and would require no

additional financial outlay, while others would use a marketing firm and may estimate up to $20,000 for this objective.

Estimated cost: $20,000

1B. Increase the win ratio on proposals to 85 percent.

The marketing department feels that with a new color laser printer and some presentation training they could meet this objective.

Estimated cost: $25,000

2A: Increase annual profits by 15 percent for the next fiscal year, to $650,000.

This objective may be achieved through a whole series of action plans, including cost cutting, asset sales, or increased revenue generating. In this case, the company chose to increase the production capability at an estimated cost of $12,000.

Estimated cost: $12,000

3A: Move into an office in downtown Mercer Island by June.

It should be fairly easy to estimate the cost of implementing this objective, if the company has already done some preliminary research on costs of office space and moving requirements.

Estimated cost: Requires research but the budget was estimated at $50,000.

The above exercise for estimating the financial gains and costs of implementation is an excellent and worthwhile management tool. Use it to clarify expectations, set realistic objectives, and make final decisions. As you work through this process, feel free to edit and change your objectives until you have clearly defined and agreed on your expectations. After clarifying your objectives, estimating your direct financial return, and estimating the costs of implementing the objectives, you will understand the overall financial impact of implementing your objectives.

Understanding the financial impact is a critical consideration in implementing your strategic plan. If you have more process-oriented objectives than you have result-oriented objectives, the company may be forced to operate in the negative this year in order to achieve its Vision in the future. Operating in the negative can be acceptable when it is planned and the decisions are justified with sound thinking and aligned with management expectations. If you are unwilling to operate in the negative, or do not have the resources to support your objectives, you may need to go back and re-prioritize your objectives to balance your budget or ensure you have the necessary resources. Setting the budget is the *Realistic* part of ensuring you have SMART objectives.

Ideally, of course, most companies prefer a balanced or positive budget. When you calculate your ROI, you will see what impact the implementation of your strategic plan is going to have on your bottom-line for the next year.

Estimating the Cost of SMART Objectives

To conclude the above example, take a look at Figure 10.2.

Based solely on the objectives in Figure 10.2, the company would be operating in the black; however, they have other objectives, including the objectives related to their annual revenue goals. You will want to integrate the budget that you develop for each of your objectives into your annual budget, which should include your sales objectives and your fixed costs. In the end, you should be able to estimate the financial picture if you successfully achieve all of your objectives.

Whether it is for a new business venture or an established profitable business, estimating the required resources is an essential part of setting SMART objectives. To balance the emphasis between investing in the future and staying financially sound in the present, you may decide to postpone some of your objectives for the following year. Once you have

> Understanding the financial impact is a critical consideration in implementing your strategic plan.

FIGURE 10.2: Estimating the Cost of SMART Objectives

1A:	Develop a marketing plan . . .
Financial gain	$0
Less cost to implement	$20,000
ROI	–$20,000

1B.	Increase the win ration on proposals to 85 percent.
Financial gain	$150,000
Less cost to implement	$25,000
ROI	+$125,000

2A:	Increase annual profits by 15 percent for the next fiscal year, to $650,000.

In this objective the financial gain is clear:

Financial gain	$97,500
Less cost to implement	$12,000
ROI	+$85,500

3A:	Move into an office in downtown Mercer Island by June.
Financial gain	$0
Less cost to implement	$50,000
ROI	–$50,000

defined your objectives, you can delegate them to individuals and involve the rest of your crew in your plans to turn those objectives into action.

❖ ❖ ❖ ❖ ❖

Congratulations!

You have learned how to use strategic decision-making tools and have successfully navigated the four-stage strategic decision-making process. We trust that you have gained many useful and valuable strategic insights. We encourage you to apply the principles and skills you have learned to strategically position your business. Other invaluable resources to assist your strategic decision-making include:

+ The *Chart Your Own Course* workbook that guides you step-by-step through the process described in this book.

+ Attend one of our *Chart Your Own Course*™ seminars or retreats.

+ Hire a licensed *Chart Your Own Course*™ facilitator.

Applied Business Solutions, Inc.
Web: www.sail2success.com
E-mail: info@sail2success.com

Index

Another tool from Applied Business Solutions, Inc.

CARYN A. SPAIN'S

CHART YOUR OWN COURSE®

WORKBOOK FOR DEVELOPING BUSINESS STRATEGY

THIRD EDITION

When you are ready to Turn Your Vision into Action, this is the resource you need! Chart Your Own Course® (CYOC) puts the theory of business strategy presented in Strategic Insights into a workbook format so you can apply it to your company for immediate results. The CYOC workbook takes you step-by-step through the strategic planning and decision-making process. Complete with dozens of worksheets, examples, and easy-to-read instructions, the CYOC Workbook is the most cost effective guide for developing a comprehensive business strategy on the market today.

CHECK OUT OUR HOT NEW WEB SITE!
http://www.appliedbizsolutions.com
Download our FREE **Motivational** Sailing Scenes **Screensaver**.
Register for an upcoming *Chart Your Own Course*® Strategic Decision-Making Retreat.

Fax: 206.329.7484 or email: info@appliedbizsolutions.com

ORDER FORM

YES, I AM A BUSINESS LEADER WHO IS READY TO DEVELOP A VIABLE AND COMPELLING BUSINESS STRATEGY! Please send me a copy of the *Chart Your Own Course*® workbook for only $60.00 plus $5.00 shipping. Washington State residents add $5.16 sales tax.

Applied Business Solutions, Inc., 1407 E. Madison St. PMB 3, Seattle, WA 98122

Number of Copies_____ (Including copies for Executive Team Members and as gifts)

Name _____ Company _____

Address _____

City _____ State _____ Zip _____

Phone # _____ Fax# _____

E-mail Address _____ Website: http://www._____

Visa/MasterCard # _____

Expiration Date _____ Signature _____

Successful Business Library

A Complete Franchise Solution.

From The Oasis Press®

Understand the nuances of running a franchise or turning your existing business into a successful franchise model. Each of these books offer unparalleled expertise in helping you make the most of operating a franchise in today's marketplace...

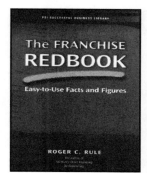

The Franchise Redbook
Easy-to-Use Facts and Figures
ROGER C. RULE

An accurate and user-friendly reference that will help determine your best franchise opportunity. While there are several other reference books available, *The Franchise Redbook* is up-to-date, comprehensive, and by far the easiest to use to determine your franchise options. The organized listings make it easy to weigh the pros and cons of the franchises within your area of interest. Ideal for selecting a franchise, doing market and comparative analysis, preparing a marketing or business plan, preparing contact lists, or doing any other research on franchises.

PAPERBACK $34.95   ISBN 1-55571-484-6
                                                750 PAGES

No Money Down Financing for Franchising

ROGER C. RULE

An essential resource for securing finances and building the foundation to a winning franchise. Broken down into three logical progressions, this book explores every resource available for franchise financing, including many methods that require no money down and explains the vital points that will prepare you in obtaining these goals.

PAPERBACK $19.95   ISBN 1-55571-462-5
                                                240 PAGES

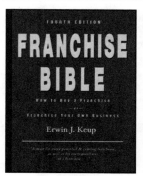

Franchise Bible, 4th edition
How to Buy A Franchise or Franchise Your Own Business
ERWIN J. KEUP

If you are thinking about acquiring a franchise or franchising your own business, this indispensable and recognized guide will tell you how to do it, and save you time and money in the process. You'll learn the advantages and disadvantages of the franchise system and familiarize yourself with the terms and concepts that are essential in operating a franchise today. A recognized, must-read if you are interested in the world of franchising.

PAPERBACK $27.95   ISBN 1-55571-526-5
                                                274 PAGES

TO ORDER CALL 1-800-228-2275 OR VISIT YOUR FAVORITE BOOKSTORE

The Oasis Press®
Successful Business Library

Tools to help you save time and money.

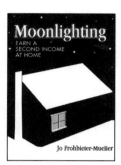

Moonlighting: Earn a Second Income at Home
Paperback: $15.95

Pages: 240
ISBN: 1-55571-406-4

It is projected that half of the homes in America are expected to house some type of business in the next few years. *Moonlighting* takes the idea of starting your own home-based business a step further. It will show you, in realistic and achievable steps, how you can initially pursue a business dream part-time, instead of quitting your job and being without a financial safety net. This confidence building guide will help motivate you by showing you the best steps toward setting your plan in motion.

Home Business Made Easy
Paperback: $19.95

Pages: 233
ISBN: 1-55571-428-5

An easy-to-follow guide to help you decide if starting a home-based business is right for you. Takes you on a tour of 153 home business options to start your decision process. Author David Hanania also advises potential business owners on the fiscal aspects of small startups, from financing sources to dealing with the IRS.

Which Business?
Paperback: $18.95

Pages: 376
ISBN: 1-55571-342-4

A compendium of real business opportunities, not just "hot" new ventures that often have limited earning potential. *Which Business?* will help you define your skills and interests by exploring your dreams and how you think about business. Learn from profiles of 24 business areas, reviewing how each got their start and problems and successes that they have experienced.

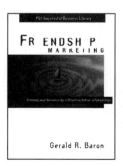

Friendship Marketing
Paperback: $18.95

Pages: 187
ISBN: 1-55571-399-8

If you have every wondered how to combine business success and personal signficance, author Gerald Baron has numerous practical suggestions. After years of working with executives and entrepreneurs, he's found that business success and personal meaning can share common ground. Using dozens of examples, he shows how building relationships is the key to business development and personal fulfillment.

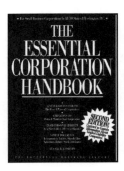

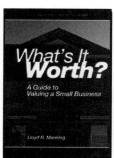

The Oasis Press®
Successful Business Library
Tools to help you save time and money.

Funding High-Tech Ventures
Paperback: $21.95

Pages: 160
ISBN: 1-55571-405-6

Pursuing a high-tech business has never been more opportune, however the competition in the industry is downright grueling. Author Richard Manweller brings a smart, in-depth strategy with motivational meaning. It will show you how to tailor your strategy to grain investor's attention. If you are looking for a financial angel, *Funding High-Tech Ventures* is the guidance you need to make the right match.

businessplan.com
Paperback: $21.95

Pages: 160
ISBN: 1-55571-405-6

Pursuing a high-tech business has never been more opportune, however the competition in the industry is downright grueling. Author Richard Manweller brings a smart, in-depth strategy with motivational meaning. It will show you how to tailor your strategy to grain investor's attention. If you are looking for a financial angel, *Funding High-Tech Ventures* is the guidance you need to make the right match.

Financial Management Techniques
Paperback: $21.95

Pages: 250
ISBN: 1-55571-405-6

Pursuing a high-tech business has never been more opportune, however the competition in the industry is downright grueling. Author Richard Manweller brings a smart, in-depth strategy with motivational meaning. It will show you how to tailor your strategy to grain investor's attention. If you are looking for a financial angel, *Funding High-Tech Ventures* is the guidance you need to make the right match.

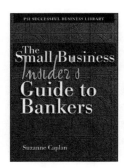

The Small Business Insider's Guide to Bankers
Paperback: $21.95

Pages: 163
ISBN: 1-55571-405-6

Pursuing a high-tech business has never been more opportune, however the competition in the industry is downright grueling. Author Richard Manweller brings a smart, in-depth strategy with motivational meaning. It will show you how to tailor your strategy to grain investor's attention. If you are looking for a financial angel, *Funding High-Tech Ventures* is the guidance you need to make the right match.

ALL MAJOR CREDIT CARDS ACCEPTED

CALL TO PLACE AN ORDER
— or —
TO RECEIVE A FREE CATALOG
1-800-228-2275

International Orders (541) 245-6502   *Fax Orders* (541) 245-6505
Web site http://www.psi-research.com   *Email* sales@psi-research.com

PSI Research   P.O. Box 3727   Central Point, Oregon   97502
U.S.A.